CO
JU

D0795795

This book sucks ass!

Dn+ even waste ur time

C-Train
(Dream Boy's Story)

and

Thirteen Mexicans

ALSO BY JIMMY SANTIAGO BACA

A Place to Stand
Healing Earthquakes
Black Mesa Poems
Immigrants in Our Own Land and Selected Early Poems
Martin & Meditations on the South Valley

C-Train
(Dream Boy's Story)

and

Thirteen Mexicans

Poems

Jimmy Santiago Baca

CONTRA COSTA COUNTY
JUVENILE HALL LIBRARY

Grove Press
New York

Copyright © 2002 by Jimmy Santiago Baca

All rights reserved. No part of this book may be reproduced in any form or by
any electronic or mechanical means, including information storage and
retrieval systems, without permission in writing from the publisher, except by
a reviewer, who may quote brief passages in a review. Any members of
educational institutions wishing to photocopy part or all of the work for
classroom use, or publishers who would like to obtain permission to include
the work in an anthology, should send their inquiries to Grove/Atlantic, Inc.,
841 Broadway, New York, NY 10003.

Published simultaneously in Canada
Printed in the United States of America

FIRST EDITION

Library of Congress Cataloging-in-Publication Data

Baca, Jimmy Santiago, 1952–
    C-train (Dream Boy's story) and thirteen Mexicans : poems / Jimmy Santiago
Baca.—1st ed.
        p. cm.
    ISBN 0-8021-3947-7
    I. Mexican Americans—Poetry.   I. Title.
PS3552.A254 C18 2002
811'.54—dc21   2002029417

DESIGN BY LAURA HAMMOND HOUGH

Grove Press
841 Broadway
New York, NY 10003

02 03 04 05   10 9 8 7 6 5 4 3 2 1

This is dedicated to my brother, Mieyo Baca,
who didn't make it, and to all you others
trying to get your lives on track.

Contents

C-Train

(Dream Boy's Story)

One

My name is Dream Boy. I dream of many things: good life, good job, good friends. There came a day when all my dreams turned into a nightmare of shattered mirrors, with each successive distortion more grotesque. But at first our guests appeared like relief workers, taking us out of our financial and emotional worries. They were welcome to our quiet one-bedroom stucco bungalow, and their arrival seemed expected, in the way that a card reader sometimes hits it right, so it seemed imprinted on my bones, fully visible at this hour on this day, and I had no choice but to follow the consequences of their visit to its ill conclusion, drawn on, I suppose in hindsight, by my youthful arrogance. I would not have believed it myself. I thought I was strong enough to say no or yes to anything offered me.

One day when Laura was about six months pregnant, we were sitting in our living room. It was evening, a cool night. I remember the rain had blackened the budding stems of flowers and the boughs of trees.

We had dreams stacked up for the future. We planned the kind of house we might build in the mountains, what kind of job she might get after completing school, and how we would raise our child. We took as much care and forethought with our coming child as a seamstress fitting a beautiful white wedding dress on a bride.

And then that night in March, Willy walked into our lives. Jorge had brought him over.

Orale, DB, Jorge had said. You remember my cousin? The one from New York?

¿Como estas? Willy said. He was chubby and genial-looking. His black hair tumbled into curls and his smile spread across his face. Right away my wife liked him. He sat on the couch and Jorge sat on the chair. Willy leaned his elbow on a black shoulder bag

beside him. He began to talk about wines and pastry delicacies. My wife, being Spanish, dove headlong into the conversation.

Jorge was giving me little signs with his eyes that he had something to say, but not in front of my wife. So I rose and went into the kitchen, and then after a minute I called for him to help me bring the wine out for my wife and Willy.

You know anybody that wants to buy coke? Jorge asked.

Maybe, depending on how good it is, I said. Offhand, I didn't know anybody. I just wanted to test some. I had quit using it a year ago, when I had met Laura, and by way of congratulating myself, I felt I deserved just a little taste.

You got some coke? I asked, back in the living room. Willy's face came alive.

He immediately unzipped his black leather shoulder bag. Another black pouch he unzipped had four ounces in it. I went into the kitchen and took a plate, a spoon, and a knife and came back. He handed me the bag and I scooped a good portion from it. I smashed it on the plate and made nice long thick lines. With a straw I had cut in half, we each took turns blowing the yellowish-white medicine into our noses. All except Laura, who didn't touch the stuff because she was pregnant.

We stayed up until three or four in the morning. Then Willy asked me if I could sell any for him. I said I could, if the price was right. He said he would return in a week. He was staying over at his cousin's house, and after that he would return to New York. He left us an ounce for $1,000 and we thanked him. After they had left, I stayed up the rest of the night talking with Laura, pouring myself more and more coke onto the plate. It was magical medicine for me. The past few months I had been feeling worthless and stuck in a pit, and it picked my spirit up.

Laura went to bed about eight in the morning and I sat in the living room, just as dawn was creeping over the Sandias. Where was I and where was my life? A sinking feeling filled me. My mind moved too fast to focus on any particular memory to give me perspective. I kept taking lines of coke and looking dumbly out the window at the yard.

We could make money on this ounce, I thought. As I looked on the plate, specks of white crystals scattered about, I felt total control over my life and good fortune coming. I would sell this and make the money needed to buy a used car. And even as I snorted more and more lines, I was certain knew I could sell the rest and make good on the ounce.

The sun warmed the windows and the day began, brimming with new opportunities. Sparrows shot across the yard; I could hear their incessant sharp sounds coming from the evergreen bushes beneath the kitchen window. Traffic increased on the street outside. Students shouldering backpacks stuffed with textbooks walked by, and I was glad I was alive today. It was my time for pleasure and leisure, for easy money and getting high. I did four or five lines now at a time. My eyes were glazed with the effects of coke pulsing in my blood, my heart beating hard with the excitement of potential achievements in the near future. Lying on the couch and staring out the window, I thought about the time when I first met Laura.

I had been working the graveyard shift at a lumberyard. Laura was a secretary there, and every morning I waited to leave until she came in. I wanted to sit with her for a moment and have a cup of coffee, see her face, enjoy her gentle company. She was a sweet woman, with small wrists, slender piano fingers, and an easy and always chuckling voice.

Her most endearing quality was how important she made me feel. She didn't pretend to be shy or flirt with me; right away she gave me as much attention as I gave her. There was some swaying light in her eyes that softened even the hardest days at work, and I looked forward to talking and being in her company.

She very quickly became the reason I went to work, and as our friendship gathered momentum she came in earlier and earlier to talk with me. I started opening myself up and telling her about my past.

I've traveled a lot, I told her. Not from any sense to see America or expand my experience, but more from a deep discontent. I went to Idaho, San Francisco, Oregon, and Montana, and I decided to settle in Denver.

What was there? Nothing, actually. Either I couldn't find any work or I didn't know how to work. All my life I've jumped from one job to the next, dishwasher to security guard to woodchopper. I enjoy the blood in my body pumping vigorously and being able to breathe in the fresh morning mountain air. I wanted freedom, what kind I don't know. I wanted to break away from the invisible cage I was trapped in, from this feeling of being caught and predestined to dream about how things could be for me. I didn't know what I wanted, but I knew I couldn't endure this day-to-day burden of wanting, desiring, dreaming, and feeling unfulfilled.

So I went. But what happened? I fell into drugs again. It was all right for a while. I never made any money, and I always abused drugs. I wanted to rid myself of my body, of this skin that kept my spirit prisoner. Doing drugs was like opening the flesh that hung around my spirit; a door opened and I was able to step outside of the constant worry and discontent.

I told Laura that on Friday she could come over to have soup with me. I made the best soup in the world. And then I would finish telling her about myself.

When Friday came, she was prompt. We sat at the table and I resumed my story.

I was working construction in Idaho, and a co-worker, Randy, asked if I could get him any weed. People always thought I was a dealer, just the way I looked; I don't know why.

Anyway, I bluffed and said I could. He could sell it, he said, and that night we made arrangements. I would get the weed and he would sell it. Well, I called a friend of mine in Texas; he said he could bring up three hundred pounds. We waited for two weeks and Tino came, trunk full of weed.

The weed business eventually introduced me to coke dealers. And I started taking coke. I quit my job and started hauling weed from Texas. To stay awake, I snorted coke. It also took away the pain of knowing I should be doing something else with my life. Taking coke gave me a rest; it blinded me to my real life, postponed responsibility.

I started off buying grams, then quarter ounces, then ounces. All for me and my friends. I wasn't making money and I wasn't thinking about my life. I was in limbo, nonexistent and numb.

Over a period of months I got burnt out. I lost control. I moved back here after that. I wanted to get away from drugs and do something right with my life.

When I arrived here, I bought a Harley. At the motorcycle shop I met the mechanic and he gave me a little coke. After that, I went to a concert and I met an old friend. I went to his house afterward and we ended up at his kitchen table snorting coke until dawn.

Nothing had changed; I was going back into the same old patterns. I was spending my days doing hustles, getting high on snort, drinking wine and whiskey, and running with ladies on the street.

One day I had set up a deal on borrowed money, and the deal fell through. I went back and told the people what had happened, and they gave me until midnight to get their money back. That's when I met you, I said.

Laura knew the rest of the story. We sipped our soup. I knew she was thinking how I had gone over to her house and told her goodbye. I was going to shoot it out with those people because I didn't have all their money. I got most of it but I still needed three hundred dollars. They wanted it all by midnight.

Laura lent me the money so I wouldn't get killed. And that night I vowed never again to befriend people like that and to leave the drug world once and for all.

But I did not. I didn't know how deep I was going to get myself in this time.

Two

In leathers and jeans, green sunglasses, hair down to my
    shoulders,
scooter tramp,
disintegrating my life—a black oil seeping back into the ground.
I smiled on my Harley as wind
ripped my life up from its roots.

I was the motion
tearing life's hinges apart, burying the ancient white voice in me
with distance and distance
as I rode away from things that connected me to myself.

And as I passed other states, I saw the life I used to live—
rakes lying in yards,
nails and screws and planks, gallons of paint, delivery trucks
roaring past me.
Chicken wire and front-yard shrubs, bricks and tires and
    trash cans.
My relationship
with them had broken down. My body was now an old mountain
and my heart an abandoned wood mill.
I left dates and times on my calendar open forever. I left contracts
    unsigned
on my kitchen table,
the door to my house ajar, knowing friends would rummage and
    salvage
what they could,
to be given back if I returned, to be kept as mementos if I didn't.

Rain rusted me, wind shredded me, sun stroked me, and moon
    pulled me forth
to broken-down boundaries
of my own self. I had ceased to be. Who I was lay in the mud
    and rotted
in the city.
I let myself die. I created an earthquake from opposite pressures;
my right and my left hand
wanted opposite things—one wanted a home and the other
    wanted open space.
My right eye saw beauty
in one woman, and my left eye saw beauty in all women. My
    right leg wanted
to rest and my left wanted to walk.

The pressure grew and I split into an earthquake. My life was a
     deep black pit
I hurled myself into,
driving down I-40 through Oklahoma at night on my Harley,
born again.

I thought all darkness was the same. I suckled and nurtured from
     the night sky
and thought the darkness
in poolroom back rooms and alleys was the same. I thought
     low-voiced
cocaine dealers were stars
dressed in black. I thought the ragged mobs were as innocent as
     field weeds
whose dreams blossomed small purple flowers
under the moonlight. I thought the darkness was the same and
     would feed me.
But in the darkness of dealers and con artists,
the glow from coins shines brighter than the moon. The polish-
     chromed cars
burn deeper than the sun on them.
They shed promises and loyalty like a dog scratching winter fur off
in summer heat.

Night's darkness was odorous with birth, while their black casual
     leather
coats smelled with the stench of death,
of always being closed within rooms, curtains drawn and doors
     locked
like casket hoods until I couldn't breathe.
After so much, now, I look a person in the face and can tell the
     different
shades of darkness.

Three

Ahh, a crystalline geyser
                    of awakening wavelets
                    of cocaine
                    dazzles
                    the heart's cut-glass leaves,
                    scintillates
                    brains with phosphorescent
                    blaze
                              of meaninglessness.

Outlaw rapper and night hustler,
I adjust my senses
like remote-control mirrors
on wealth;
under adrenaline storms of neon bulbs
on downtown streets,
I lounge in showroom metallic flash;
my blower-motor brain
flicked to high,
I scam grams and sniff.
                    Ahh, a crystalline geyser. . . .

Four

I dropped out
of high school and drilled my black Mustang
through southern
California orange groves,
radio full blast; leaned back,
I glided aged border towns

from Juarez to T.J.—
Joplin wailing blues
and Hendrix hipped guitar
wanged my psychedelic trips.
Tires screeched and bumper
sparked asphalt like Fourth of July sparklers
from the weight of a packed trunk
of plastic-wrapped kilos of Acapulco gold,
I hauled from Mejico
to Burque, Denver, San Diego, and Oregon.

Boys my age clucked milk
in cafeterias while I salted my back hand,
emptied a shot glass of tequila, licked the salt,
bit a lemon wedge, then tipped the barmaid fifty—
in my duel-tank CD'd Mustang
I forged my fate in the fury
of a ravenous thirst to be somebody;
I wore tattered knee-shredded pants,
cotton plaid shirt
threadbare at elbows,
washed in park lakes
where I slept and ate and lived
in between business and concerts,
played my harmonica and beat congas,
drank tequila and saluted la vida loca.

While others my age
humped over biology and astronomy books
in dorms, downy feathered cocaine flakes
volcanized seismic meanings
for me and avalanched
me downward
into five feet eleven inches
of molten pleasure,
shimmering immediate metamorphosis.

*   *   *

While others drifted
in the happy thoughtless pause
between teenage years and maturity,
my business associates
offered lines and explained,
"Buy a half and I'll front you a half,"
promising security
in the maddening chaos of the world.
And while college kids my age
high-stepped on coffee and aspirin,
I snorted three–four grams a night
in sleepless ecstasy, until my eyes
were frost-chilled windows
diluting whatever was viewed
to fuzzed outlines and hazy mayhem.

Friends drew pistols on friends.
Bic caps were used to sample the latest load.
Fear and paranoia sounded warning shots
over snow-capped glaciers
of glittering Peruvian pebbles.
I whizzed into barren, bleak landscapes
on no food or sleep for days,
unable to remember where
I came from, where
I was going.
Sounds of screams—
Where am I?
How do I get back?
Hurling furniture
in a fit of fury,
I gashed walls,
and a mad mood of doom
darkened my words and gestures
with measured caution.

                        ✻   ✻   ✻

I changed friends,
quit even marginal visits
to those not into cocaine.
All-night snorting.
Where did I park my car?
My keys?
What day is today?
Accused overnight women
of stealing my stash,
coke grains in my nostrils,
lips cracked from lack of vitamins,
eyes stained red with sleepless
curtain peeks and side glances,
my body trembling and jittery
with addiction.

I tore out drawers,
turned over beds,
checked cabinets,
closets, and at last found it,
unwrapped the tinfoil, chopped
long white lines on a plate,
and snorted in—
letters on the kitchen countertop
unopened,
bills unpaid, doorbells and telephone calls
unanswered.

Five

The lies started
because who I was
couldn't take the betrayal of what I had done
to those I loved, so I created a compartment
where the liar existed, a small dark cave where
he cannibalized his heart and soul—
kept away from others—
isolating himself in a house of lies,
going into the world only to drink and drug
and fuck, waking up in the morning remembering nothing,
no words, no behavior, wallowing
in murky alcohol grogginess that padded the wounds,
the hurts, the numbing pain of life.
How the weight got heavier with each day, each encounter—
maybe it was rage, maybe fear, maybe the inadequacy
of being flung into the world without skills
or words to communicate my heart.
How it went on, drearily fucking, faceless, bodiless,
mindless,
caught in sordid, dizzying reel toward oblivion
until the character I created to contain
the lies, deception, drunkenness, violence,
the obscene indulgence, started
cracking the walls that separated us, crumbling
foundations, crushing the door down
until the character's venom seeped into the person
who wanted it kept away, ugly and toxic
veins of lies trickling into my clean words,
darkening my bright eyes, paling my cheeks
until I was haunted by an evil usurpation
of my being, consumed by a gluttonous appetite
until I was what I hated, loathing myself,
all my expression fulfilling its order

to abandon my soul, my heart,
miring myself in lies, bathing in my own foul deceptions
of all I loved and respected.
How I became a drunk, an addict, each day and every hour
my heart festering howls for more and more
until I lived for the drug, lived to get high,
to lose myself in the darkest abyss of addiction.
Parts of myself died, crawled away into holes,
my spiritual life burned like paper in the wind,
my compassion hardened like old crumbs
of bread, and within me
the dogs of wrath and condemnation snarling, raging
day in and day out, full of contradictions,
dying and living, free and imprisoned,
feeling and insensitive, two people,
two lives, guttering away
in the sewer of addiction.

Six

I bought a round-trip ticket
on the Cocaine Express,
a white train that speeds
through the night. The porters are dressed in white coats
and offer you lines on silver platters.
It stops at every town
to pick up passengers—
shopkeepers, dentists, lawyers, judges—
from every sector of society.
We keep going, and the travel guide explains
to us, "Man, if you off a quarter,
I'll front you half." The world can be ours, he says.

We go deeper and deeper into the snowy hills,
up glaciers, until there are no signs of life.
Just the snorting and ecstatic breathing of the train.
We are sleepless.
Soon a few passengers start to scream in the car
behind ours. To appease our fears and paranoia,
        porters hand out glittering rocks,
                golden razor blades,
                        and golden spoons.
We eat the same meal
we have been eating now
for days, months maybe.
When one of the rich passengers asks
where we are going,
the porters don't know. The train speeds and speeds,
whizzing past barren countryside.
It's been dark for a long time. The sun has stopped shining.

Suddenly, after months, maybe years, no one can remember,
the train abruptly collides. The sound of screams fills my ears.
        Where are we? someone asks.
        How do we get back?
        All around us we see the beautiful white snowy land
        no one can get out of.
A month later maybe, for we have all lost count of days,
the passengers start eating each other.
        Some hear echoes and voices.
        Some run raving mad into the white wilderness.
        Others fling themselves off cliffs.

Seven

I boarded the Cocaine Express
and out the frosted window, as it was pulling away,
I saw my wife and child waving at me.
I passed through Tucson by a friend's house.
He stood out in the graveled road
roaring louder than the train's engines
for me to jump.
I looked back at his clapboard house
bordered with a paint-peeled leaning picket fence,
shaded with trees and wild bushes,
the windows of his house deep blue
and the roof sagging
from the heat of the desert.

> The wheels turned fast as fans,
> dispersing my soul
> behind like blue air.

At small-town stations along the way
I pressed my face to the window,
numbly staring at friends waving me off.

I invented myself
like a painter splashing my destiny on canvas
in red passion,
blue sorrow,
green nostalgia,
yellow joy.

> I let instinct
> plummet me down,
> building momentum until I hurled headlong
> on the Cocaine Express, cocaine courier
> with a white scroll in my pocket
> whose message was death.

Eight

Driving I-40—
Snow-packed one-lane through Ohio,
four inches of ice packed on truck grill
and headlights—I stopped
in a train-track mountain town
to hack with a hammer at the ice.

Dealing weed,
I dream of safer work.
Waiting,
waiting in dark rooms for money,
for a phone call,
in barrooms for a stranger,
waiting, waiting, waiting.

In a nightclub my dreams float on the air,
smoke rings blown from red lips,
from black-mustached lips, scarred lips,
pursed lips, thin and full voluptuous lips,
from them all under blue and red lights,
my dreams spiral and thin into the perfumed
sweaty-smelling air.

I throw my freedom to the wind
like corn grains to chickens in the yard.
Wolf in the woods on the run,
misfit gypsy zoot-suiter,
night raider,
cloaked sickle reaper,
            in crash pads,
            in stolen cars,
            on streets at midnight
            lined with thieves and whores,
            among the scarred drunkards

on the savage highways,
with the desperate, the dissolute,
the damaged and disdained,
I live in places
where there is no light.

Cocaine
on my kitchen table;
I take a chunk and scrape
a pile on a plate. With a straw
I snort all day. At evening
I hear noises outside the curtains.
I see shadows pass by me. My eyes
stark with terror, my mind
a dog hit by a car,
my tongue cut off,
soon I shuffle on knuckles along the pavement.

Nine

Dealing myself out
to the wind,

dealing myself out
to the hot summer,

dealing myself out
an ad
in slick leathers
with a hard dick,
luring ladies
with my outlaw rap,

*   *   *

cartoon
falling along the way
down cliffs
tied to the weight of nightmare.

Ten

Doing cocaine:
piano keys move by themselves
doors open by themselves
lamps shake by themselves
voices quake with laughter
down empty hallways—
my mind blinded by white light.

Eleven

I travel with the hooded ones
along steep and narrow trails
close to the moon. A line of us,
mournful and violent, climbing
always to distance ourselves from society.
We look below to the cities,
our faces hidden deep in our cowls,
and we snarl at the damage
we impose on ourselves.
Then,
we reach into our cloak pockets,
open our plastic bags, and snort our coke.

We dance and howl,
fling cloaks and sandals off,
lunge body on body, flinch with pleasure,
let the heart and mind go like pebbles
down the sharp descent, bouncing off into oblivion,
as our bodies butt, grunt, merge
bone to bone, with bestial indulgence.
Rebel sect praising our White Queen,
with chapped lips and stuffed noses,
in mad delirium—
in the morning, nothing is left of us,
our hearts and minds translucent
leaves eaten by insects.

Twelve

I got sucked in as easily as a lumbering cow
sloshes in a quicksand pond.
I got sucked into the cesspool,
flushed down into the murky stench of addiction,
where coke was the medicine
to make me invisible, to help me forget my life;
where coke had become my ghost
thrashing my insides with nightmares, howling at me,
defiling my existence with its ivory
chains around my hands and its ring
around my nose.
I saw double days, triple faces,
and heard the air crack, felt fury in my bones;
my mind crumbled promises
like crackers, and my heart became a poisonous pool
I drank from, becoming delirious
and chaotic, promising myself I would quit tomorrow,

tomorrow and tomorrow,
raving at imagined things, ravenous for coke,
glutted and swollen with my medicine,
to ease the forest fire burning my life down,
to ease the agony
making ash of all I planted,
deaf to the growls of thornbushes in open fields
that pulled my pant legs back to stop me from going
to my connection's house.

Thirteen

Tired of $2.50-an-hour jobs,
tired of wondering where I was going to live,
how I was going to live.
I crumpled up my soul
and burned it,
because I could not eat it,
could not take it down to the utility companies
to pay my gas, electric, and water bills,
could not stand outside my landlord's house
and offer it instead of money,
so I got a job hauling marijuana.

At school people told me, "Keep away from me,"
and looked askance when our eyes met
crossing the cobblestone courtyard.
During hours I should have been in class
I was in the bathroom snorting coke
with a rolled-up dollar bill,
killing myself,
insulating my heart
to keep me warm from the cold waters of life.

Friends withdrew.
I felt the pain of a stray dog
kicked from every doorstep to stray
in the night down endless roads.

Fourteen

Cocaine gives the body an awareness, an alarm,
a bizarre excitement. It expects.
The body is urgent, anxious. The mind becomes
a cloud in which saints ride
as medieval paintings depict the arrival of angels.
The believers become fanatics
bringing upon the barrio and slum neighborhoods
their new religion.

The dealers are in euphoria and ecstasy,
their raiments are the finest silk,
and a coterie of disciples crowds them
as they go about blessing the pagans
working in mines, in mills, or in fields—

They go about giving prophecies
of a beautiful world,
their followers poor, forced to give all they have,
beaten if they do not pay tribute.

Fifteen

Lalo—nice brick house and pottery business—
indulged my desperation
with twenty-five pounds of Acapulco gold.
I drove east,
carrying this earth hair that enchanted millions,
an outlaw voodoo man.
I ran a roadblock in the Texas panhandle,
gambling my freedom and my life for twenty gunnysacks of weed.
Freedom from responsibility,
no job, no home, no land, no bills, no friends,
just the lonely abysm of curving roads.
Like the white laboratory rat injected with test chemicals
I arrived at my destination and rang the bell,
pulled the lever, and out came my coke.
I had freedom, the kind of freedom
that destroys children, blackens teeth, opens wounds,
and kills.
Every car that passed my window I suspected,
every man that entered restaurant bathrooms
after me I suspected,
every headlight drawing nearer in my rearview mirror
on the dark highway I suspected,
every cop that passed me I suspected,
every click on the phone was a tap,
and with every one of these suspicions
a knife came down from the air in front of me
and cut a red chunk of meat from my heart
until it was a ragged piece of trash-can meat
flies buzzed around.
In grimy soiled sheets I slept
from Juarez to New York
in squalid shacks festering with broken pipes,
cockroaches, and rats, men and women
laid back with cool raps,

beads and incense, guns and knives,
all of us driven forth by the white tide,
foaming from our guts,
with cracked lips and sniffles, glazed eyes,
drowning in blue delusions.

Sixteen

I was clinging to a floating log
circled with alligators
down the swamp drug world.
The apes in suits watched
and snakes dangled from limbs overhanging the banks.
I could hear Bobby's agonized cries
in the jungle
as they speared him and Louie's scream of pain
as the cannibals cut his throat.

When a month later you brought a whole tribe
of warriors to hunt me down, I stood
with my loaded .32, frightened and sick,
and yelled to you all, Come on and die!
No one came. Maddened with desperation,
my eyes crazed,
my body convulsing with war drums,
I yelled to the world, Come on and let's die!

Seventeen

I wanted the taste of darkness
on my tongue,
and the dark rage of desperation
to clothe me.
I threw my soul on the table
like a jack of spades,
and said, Let's play.
My days were a stack of white chips
and my nights a stack of black chips.

Dealer man,
when you came in your leather coat,
camera bag slung over shoulder,
curly black hair,
and moons below your eyes
from sleepless cocaine nights,
you threw ounces on the table and said, Let's play.

It was just a game
and months later, looking out my window
at night, I wondered what had happened to me.
My bones had become black sticks
and my soul white ashes. With each gray breath
smoke spiraled
into the cold October night,
like the aftermath of a city burned to the ground.

I growled and gnawed at myself
in a world of charred horizons,
smoldering skies, and embering trees.
I blinded my eyes,
numbed my touch,
deafened myself to a still afternoon

with green umbrellas of trees,
lost scent of the morning-watered gardens.

I became a brute with a heavy goblet
guzzling whiskey,
slurring obscenities in whore dens,
burying my senses in white sand,
my eyes two jades laid in the grave.

In the sweet darkness of my soul
cocaine fell like a Christmas snowfall,
and in countless apartments I rose
from soiled beds and opened the curtains
to see death outside.

Eighteen

Through southern California orchards
sweltering mulch, tree limbs tuned
like strings giving off fat red notes
of apples, always on the road
we glided beneath the long narrow arbors
of nameless trees, radio full blast;
cranking the engine, we roared on.
At bronzed borders
we had to show our arms to La Migra
who inspected them for needle marks.
The engine raged across the desert,
until in San Diego, up a ramp to Ocean Beach,
the LSD shocked us and the ramp became a flying saucer,
and we looked at the blue horizon,
thinking we were shooting off into space.

Lorenzo, the THC you sold to army boys
at the base in Arizona
had us bellyaching with laughter the next morning
when half the base didn't show for reveille.
They were out,
dazzled by the chemical, running naked across the
    compound,
screeching about devils.
Dancer, your eyes
were always screened with smoke. Shaggily dressed,
always smoking joints, ashtrays glutted with roaches,
buzzing off to Denver to catch Hendrix.
I envied that gloating leer on your face, always there
as if you were privy to a secret wisdom
marijuana consoled you with. Tons back-to-back
was your pride in life.
Gato, you told me your first experience
with drugs was along the Texas–Mexican border
where you polished tourist shoes—
made them look like turtles just emerged from water,
as they crawled down the sidewalk
leaving wet marks behind
from your sweat that poured over them.
You had one can filled with polish
and the other filled with neatly rolled joints.
As you grew older, you started pulling fifty pounds
across the Rio Grande on inner tubes
and selling weed up north for $300
a pound.

What did we all have in common
after years of dealing? Fear and mistrust,
rip-offs, guns, dark mornings counting crumpled dollars.
I was used to failing, expected to fail,
and I purposely soured my sweet tongue with curses,
maddened my peacefulness
with nightly raids into howling beer-chugging parties.

I fulfilled the destiny others expected of me,
became the brutal beast
gnawing myself
into
something bad and evil and feared.
And after years of living
in this infected
acceptance
of whining friends who enjoyed
my suicide,
I decided one day that there would be no show.
They would all have to go home and bite their hands. I was not a
   bad man,
and I dropped my sword and left the arena.

Nineteen

My life weed willows in snowmelt
caving in sandy sides of my years—
              I swim between
              toward that sluice gauge awaiting my arrival,
              where the huge mastiff of my spirit sopping wet
              slops water everywhere
              shaking life off
              and curls before a warm fire and snores.
I remember a man walking up the sidewalk
to my back door, a soft man.
What happened to this man
I was supposed to be, and why did I become this man
              limping in from war,
              hand-slapping five and wrestling
              pistol-packing warriors on the patio,
              nursing my whiskey and cocaine,

guffawing loudly enough to wake the neighbor's dogs,
retelling stories with gangsters
about near-death encounters with DEA?
It shouldn't have been like this.
I watch leaf light at the window and listen
to horses lap water at the trough,
vigilant pheasants peck in soft weeds—
glad he is coming back,
having laid a moon wreath in the snow,
glowing with the warrior's death,
snowflake fingerprints melting,
heart-coal in my rib grate,
radiant as my woman and I
make love, grow hooves and wings, and invoke
from the warrior his angel form
in the baptismal mud bed,
browning my pulse a pepper seed
that sprouts green tendrils from my limbs
filled with hot light.

Twenty

I walk this afternoon
to an adobe house not far from here.
I go on long walks every day and end here
and wonder
at the way things have been left undone, half finished.
Resembles my life
so much.
Two depressions
where mud bricks were mixed with straw and patted,
left with crumbly bricks askew and rounding under rain and wind.
I sit on a rock and eat my burrito.

Off to the side a spindly cottonwood
pencil-thin sapling;
on one brittle twig a faded red
ribbon is tied—for luck I guess—
from another a small green leaf sprouts
wide and long as my fingernail.
It starts to sprinkle on the sapling sprig
and me,
both of us with one leaf out
amid the ruins trying to survive.

Twenty-one

I must call back that part of me
            extinct as the falcon was.

If I held my arm out in the field
and stood there
swinging the bloody chunk of my heart around
on a length of leather
would it circling high out of sight see me
with its sharp brown eye
and dive to my arm?
            It does not trust or know me anymore.
If that part of me is listening tonight
I am here for you, if you hear falcon soul
return to me.

I go searching for you in the fields,
waiting patiently.

            How does one persuade that part of oneself
            to return,

that part that spoke truth and found beauty
in each day?

Climb back into the rubble of myself
since your departure.

That whirring at my ear I sometimes hear,
wing flurries at my ear,
is my falcon skimming over me.

Where do our spirits go when we maim them?
Falcon shrieked in my clutch,
maddened by opium stains on fingertips,
cocaine in blood and liquor on my breath.

       I tied hood cowl over its eyes
       so it wouldn't see what I was doing
       and placed it in the cage of my brain.
       I tore its claws out, cut its feathers,
       destroyed its nest, blinded it, grounded it,
       and one night after abusing myself, I awoke,
       found the cage open
       blood spots on my hands
       cuts on my face—
       Falcon had freed itself
       and left me an empty cage.

I do not think the good man is extinct.
If I am truthful and honorable
and live with integrity
on a morning walk
I will place my hands to shade my eyes
from the sun one day,
       see it circling again above me,
       and I will let my arm out;
       it will dive down in a majestic roar
       of feathers

and sit on my forearm,
talons tight around my flesh;
then
I will surrender to it,
keeping my promise for a healthy life.

I feel wind on my face
and remember my flight. . . .
O falcon, loosen your wings again,
and return. . . .

Twenty-two

Once you helped
Tranquelino plow his acre, Ortega plant his chili,
and Olivio repair his house.
You were always there for mothers worried why their sons
had not come yet; there when cops
came to arrest a neighbor—
you had been a boxing champion at seventeen,
and then you gave it up to build Saint Ann's Church. You worked
all year on that project. Smooth, bronze-browed,
you'd cock your baseball cap up
when I passed and yelled *Marcelino!* You'd smile, wave,
and return to hammering.
How surprised I was at times
when I came to visit you at night, to find you
reading poetry,
and even more surprised when we sat together and you spoke
eloquently on the need for more Chicanos to write books
about our beautiful life and barrios.
You held your children like cradling a new young harvest of corn
    in your hands,

thanking the sun for their bright eyes,
for their smooth tongues lapping brown words out,
how you stuck your head out after rain
and sniffed the air, commenting
Oh, I love the smells of rained dirt of my barrio!

And then it started—
screaming at your wife, Josefina,
always hesitant while before you were openhearted,
the walls gashed from furniture you had thrown in a mad fit of fury,
bragging about your quality of coke,
absent from home for days and days,
your children weeping all the time and disobeying their mother,
the bad mood of doom darkening your home,
then buying a pistol, changing your friends, the secrecy and side
    glances,
quitting work on the church,
the dazzled glare in your eyes every time I came to visit,
your truck overturned in a canyon,
the measured calm in your gestures and words replaced by agitation
and nervous strain,
sleeping until noon every day instead of up at sunrise,
all night snorting, selling grams to outlaws all hours of the night,
the paranoia and suspicion, forgetfulness.

And then you started making promises
you never kept,
hiding your stash of coke for yourself, doing it
when Josefina went to the store.
Bulldogging Josefina into a corner, in a rage, demanding
she tell you where she hid your stash,
eyes stained red
from lack of sleep,
your body trembling and jittery,
and sometimes when I came to see you, you'd ransack drawers,
under beds, cabinets, bottles, shoes, books,
everything in the house searching for a fix,

and then you fucked Josefina for the physical pleasure only,
forcing her at times to spread-eagle,
her face contorted with pain and confusion.

I never abandoned you, Marcelino,
never contradicted you in restaurants
when you told others how everything was all right,
how life had been good to you.
You paid the tab for everyone everywhere you went,
and then, weeping one night
when I came to visit, you grabbed my arm in desperation,
and vowed to quit.
                          The dark day fell
                          like a black wall
                          cutting you off
                          from the rest of us.
                          Months passed and you
                          refused to see anyone.
                          You disconnected your phone
                          and when I passed your house
                          there was a feeling of loss in it,
                          as if someone had died.
Then I saw your truck
at Merlinda's café one morning.
I parked my car and walked in.
When I saw your face, calm and sincere,
your baseball hat cocked to one side,
I knew you made it. I sat down and wept
my love for you, tears streaming down into my coffee cup,
glistening my hands
that kept rising to clutch your shoulders, brother.

Twenty-three

This time last year,
first week of September
I stood in the airport lobby
next to the baggage-claim elevator
circulating luggage.
When my brown box with a kilo came around
I let it swing past me several times,
looking at faces in the crowd
to detect a narcotics agent.

This year in my room
I look forward instead of behind me.
I look with a sense of renewal
at the world. I have no need to turn from faces now.
I have no fear of what's behind me
or what I carry in my shoulder bag. I go about
freely as a stray German shepherd barking at birds.

This time last year
I cut the plastic bag of coke and laid out
finger-thick lines on my table.
I looked out the window fearful of passing cars.
In my friend's face I saw the cold light of a lie
when he told me how much he had to pay for it.
Things hidden in his face, in the yellow cracks of teeth,
the grease and meat of a lie, and a still money-hungry man.
The sun outside had the dazzle
of a white-walled interrogation room.

This year sunlight filters through the kitchen door screen.
The house is quiet.
This time last year my life was decomposing.
There was not enough money to eat,
pay the bills, or buy wood for the stove.

Everything went into my nose. The only heat that came
wore blue and carried guns,
or struck my body with a fever for more dope.

This time last year, there was no place I didn't go
not high—
down to the local store, out back to work on the chicken coops,
to look at old trucks my neighbor was selling—
my eyes icicles.

Early mornings now I shiver outside
from the cold coming from the north.
Mice and centipedes skitter
by my boots as I lift old boards from a pile,
carry them half an acre,
and drop them where I'm building a back-porch deck.
Plumes of sawdust from my circular saw,
burnt aromas from my steel bit
drilling holes in my pickup-bed trailer hitch,
the constellations of dirt and dust that scatter in the air
over my hair and clothes as I knock down an old
barn wall, as it collides with the ground,
all these are like medicine my grandmother
spooned into me when I was ill with a cold.
These are manly medicines—
the sun and sky and earth mix with ailing
properties of my soul: an enclosed seed
that sucks up the dust and sweat from my brow to blossom
a distinct kind of pride in living.

Winding dirt roads, leaning fences,
the aromas of the black decaying bosque,
the soft fluid sounds of wind brushing cottonwood leaves,
old men pedaling 1940s bicycles,
Mexicans with bundles over shoulders searching for a place to work,
walking down Isleta, amazed at the Estados Unidos,
the children snipping flowers from overhanging

rosebushes with wingers and old women sweeping front steps,
the garrulous grouchy sounds of ancient tractors sputtering
down the road, the Monte Carlo low-riders,
lords of dignity, tattooed arms and chest,
and chickens crowing and cows bellowing—
aside from all this beauty,
I blinded myself with drugs and whiskey,
convulsing on overdoses during night-long death rituals.

Now I look back. My efforts to change myself,
recourse the carvings of my destiny
that sent me flooding down the abysms of my own sunlit beauty
into dark beauty, a beauty of shadows and fear—
efforts edged daily with desperation,
with the rustling sounds of thieves come to steal my own willpower,
efforts without substance, only need, I needed
to change by sheer force of what could be tomorrow,
of who I could form myself into.
My efforts to stand off my addiction,
were green stands of cornstalks bending in a hurricane.

Twenty-four

Dealer man
you ever think about my dead friends?
Diamonds on each finger,
Lincoln Continental, telling us you had no money
yet the bank bricks cracked
with your heavy weekly bankroll.
Telling me at your kitchen table
how I was special, you would work only with me,
coming over every week to collect your money.
Always sniffing, always low-voiced,

always a gleam in your blue eyes.
Self-important, parading as an intellectual, artist,
diplomatic, transcontinental traveler,
whore supplier, and luxury maniac,
carrying a .45 and attended by two bodyguards.
                    I got news for you.
                    You never impressed me. I needed my medicine
                    but could not afford it. So I supplied
                    myself by selling.
What happened to your son
who tells you to go to hell,
who throws dishes against the wall like you
and coughs up mimicking you in the morning over the toilet?
Everything is cool,
just you, just you, I heard so many times, why?
                    Because I was for real, not the money,
                    the affluence, the baby dolls
                    you could snap a finger and get,
                    not the power to have people killed or beat up—
I did my own dirty work,
appearing at your house by myself one night
to ask why you beat up a friend of mine—
I turned the table on you, styled out in jeans and leathers,
arriving at your house with thirty cents
and on your dresser in your bedroom there lay ten g's to blow.
                    What I did mind
were the holstered gangsters threatening us.
I minded their meanness and starving spirits,
the lies they told,
the secrecy that divided us and made us suspect each other.
With us, it was free travel, free food and lodging,
meeting new friends, free of problems.
For them it was guns, strength in numbers,
diamonds, and wealth.
And slowly we became the victims
of their appetites.
                    Indio got popped in Old Town selling to a narco—

Davil got popped in a parking lot—
Andrew turned his car over on Coors and was dead—
Neto lost his daughters to pimps in Chicago—
El Negro had his house taken away—
Ronnie had his throat cut—
Gordo came back to Dallas flat broke and spiritless;
he wanted no more from life, except to be left alone.

We had all seen too much.
We found the world was made out of people stabbing each other,
out of night hours where plans were drawn
for the murder of friends, for rip-offs, for abandoning trust.
We found the world
was littered with dead friends, the world had become a battlefield,
with no room for us who just played at being dealers.
          We divided. I became an addict
          to ease my pain with coke.
We risked it all
and we lost ourselves.
You stood alone
and laughed at using us, sneered behind your door
when one of us died or got popped.
Don't expect when we see you in your new car and bodyguards
to be our friend as before—
don't expect anything from us because we are no one.
          We now try to fill the emptiness
          we created. We now piece our lives together
          with hard memories, mean memories,
          memories we would like to change but cannot.

Twenty-five

The Dark Side of the Moon

1
The poet drives his pain
through the moon's heart
like a sparrow's beak
in the soft ripe peach.

2
The addict's needle marks
are dead moons
in the wings of the moth
that, in its blind defiance,
orbited too close to the flame
and could not free itself from the burning light.

3
On the north side
of my house, looking out the window,
to a place in the yard
where the air is bruised with cold
and the sun never shines—
stones and dust grow there,
surrounding a twig
dreaming of a single sunray.

4
In the heat of an ex-lover's memory,
my sadness is a leafless apricot tree
at the end of summer,
whose branches rake the ground
clawing fallen fruit
for one that's not shriveled.

Twenty-six

When the mind starts to forget special moments
in one's life, and you're comparing
your deterioration to others, healthier than you,
who never smoked or did drugs or stayed awake for days
routinely; even imagining
what you might look like in a coffin—
> whether there'll be anyone there to mourn you,
> will your color be right,
> starched and pressed,
> the collar on the satin pillow
> there'll be no need then to wonder about evenings
> with your lover, when you quarreled,
> staying at the apartment she was house-sitting,
> being with her—
dreams came to me like a piano playing in a dark alley
the notes soft as a nurse's hands rubbing my sore muscles,
and in another dream I'm lying in bed
watching lovers, when the meaning of happiness
comes with clarity, and the piano notes are sad,
when in the dream the woman you love
> gets up beside you
> and leaves,
> when the evil of lust
> promises
> you happiness
and instead has you walking alone in the cemetery
under the leafless branches,
wondering why the previous night when we went out to eat
I got drunk and was cruel to you,
and later at the apartment you left me snoring in bed,
and went driving around the city,
the snow piled six–seven inches in the street,
banked up on the sides as snowplows
trucked through the sparkling dark,

and you gripping the steering wheel, gloved, capped,
coated, breathing fog on the windows,
numb with sorrow, weeping
          to understand the snow, what love is,
          and how the snow that moment surrounded you
               with its chill love,
          its pure white prayer for salvation, for refuge
reflecting a silence you absorbed
while driving me later to the airport,
both of us knowing in our silence it would take time
to heal the wounds, the fear,
to trust again,
and I went up the elevator stairs
to a plane toward home, without looking back,
my heart buried beneath the snow and ice
          beneath snow, it cracks
          the frozen asphalt
          with palpitations
          wandering in all directions,
looking for love, for a place to break free
through the ice, into the warm season
of a woman's love.

The streetlamp glows dimly
in the empty parking lot,
its orb of light
reflected off the crystalline snow of our silence
when you drove me to the airport—
          a few businessmen in trench coats, scarves, and gloves
          track across the snow, toward empty buildings
          lulled into a dead sleep by the snowstorm.

Twenty-seven

At eight
my uncle lures them with grain in a pail
and then shoots one as white and black brothers
guzzle their brother's blood in the trough.

At ten I walk the chop-block streets
with a rooster's-tail strut
razored for a fight: life
a broken fire hydrant
flooding streets with blood.

In opulent estates,
fountains gazelle and bridal-train gardens drain
abundantly over spear-tipped walls.
Grecian statues offer laureled wisdom
to butlered adults with paperweight hearts
who answer the burning and gunning of America
by building more prisons.

Nobody cares what I'll find to eat or where I'll sleep.
Under streetlights throwing dirt clods
at a hornet's nest, unafraid of being stung,
I vow to avenge my poverty,
to gash unmercifally with a bicycle chain
spineless attorneys taking advantage of my misery,
rob executives in limousines
sampling heroin off a hooker's thighs,
mug pretty brokers with golden smiles
whose gutter glares condemn me,
and all the chumps
who never cracked a soup-line biscuit
or had a court gavel crush their life,
should know I plan violent schemes against you,

*　　*　　*

pray
saints melt my pain red hot,
I'll hammer sharp to take you down
to darkness where I live
and impale your heads
on La Virgen de Guadalupe's moon sickle.

Twelve years old. I am no good,
dime-bagging Peruvian flakes,
inhaling a glue rag.
With all your police and prison sentences,
you can't chase me from the street
or stop me from selling drugs,
because in my square white paper
lives God—I deal God—who gives reprieve
from earthly hell and makes me feel good,
gives me hope and self-esteem,
and transforms despair to a cocaine heaven,
until I'm killed or OD
like other homeboys trashed
on a stack of county jail corpses,
who understood life was a sewer grate,
their dignity poured down with discarded litter,
where crack creates light when all one has is darkness.

Crack is God
when hopeless days bury me
under rock piles of despair,
blocking me from feeling anymore,
breaking my heart into pieces of NOTHING.
I am is no good and preach NOTHING door-to-door,
a strong kid full of NOTHING,
from NOTHING do I ask a blessing,
to NOTHING do I pray, hope NOTHING
forgives my wrongs and NOTHING
helps when I take vengeance on you.

*   *   *

Now fourteen,
beneath a moon above the sportscaster's booth,
at the outdoors boxing coliseum,
after crowds go home and the ring is removed,
I shadowbox invisible opponents
and raise my hand as champion to the moon.
I join homeboys against a rival gang,
skip bleachers over handrails out of breath,
and hold court in the field with bats, pipes, chains,
brass knuckles, and guns,
in a game where every kid has to hold a five-ace winning heart,
or die with a poker player's bluffing hand—
because death is nothing but an eight-ball roll on the break.

My life is a Babe Ruth pop-up,
sailing beyond the rival gang's catch, hopscotching crime-
chalked sidewalks, fleeing police over backyard fences
from guard dogs barking,
down scuffed alleys where clapping windows and shutting
doors applaud me,
sliding under a stripped-car home plate, hearing the news:
Jo-Jo and Sparky got shot,
I X their names off building scorecard walls for dead.

At sixteen,
I'm a brown fighting get-down impromptu warrior,
lip-pursed oohing fevered to defy,
clicking tap shoes on sidewalks,
Chi-chi-chi-cano, heel to toe, chin chest,
Chi-chi-chi-cano,
T-shirt rolled to bare midriff, pomade hair back,
low-hugging hip khakis,
inked cross on right hand,
bandanna'd top button
tied on my Pendleton, lean and mean,
haunting you with my gangster signs.

✻　✻　✻

I learned my history
around water-bucket talk,
listening to mule-tongued growers
mutter holy whys they barbwired our lands off,
clacking my hoe in grower's dirt
on skulls and bones of my people
murdered and buried in chains.
Under a branding-hot noon
I cut lettuce for bronc-buckled
soft-palmed landowners
posing as frontiersmen,
their steerhorn Cadillac radios
tuned to religious broadcast
blaring glory to their godliness
as they loom over me.
"God hates you, spic. God hates you!
You're dirt, boy, dirt! Even dirt grows weeds,
but you, you're dirt that don't grow nothing but more dirt!"

Beat purple at age nine,
wood paddle whizzing
butt bullet stings,
I touch washcloth to welted bruises
on thigh, leg, back and wince under the shower nozzle,
cursing life.
My heart the severed head of an outlaw
pickled in a jar of liquor and drugs
to numb the hurt.
Purging the shame for being born,
OD'd, stabbed, and shot,
wanting to believe I was bad.
It was better than falling into darkness
where nothing existed but more darkness.
and I wanted to exist even as dirt, as no-good dirt.

At nineteen, trying to rebuild my life,
I got the urge to get high and did—

put pistol to my head and played roulette,
my bloodshot drunkard's eye seething rage
that my guardian angel didn't want me dead.

The dirt yard pleads for my daughter's laughter.
Her tricycle treads scribble
You are always gone
in whiskey and drugs,
never here to play or help me grow.

No heat, light, or food,
my baby's crying
chisels on the headstone of my bones
her need for a father,
wobble to a stop
when I pick her from the crib,
inhale her milky aroma,
patting and kissing her,
walking her back and forth
in the cold living room,
warming her in my skin heat,
breathing warmth on her,
holding her to my chest,
humming a deep-chest hymn,
"Bendito, bendito, bendito sea Dios,
los angeles cantan y daban a Dios. . . ."

"Blessed, blessed, blessed is the Lord,
the angels sing and give to the Lord. . . ."
Her tiny hand flexes, a wing
unwrinkling from cocoon for flight,
fossilized in the stone of my arms.
I am two men with one life—
I love her, care about her feelings,
want to live at home, be a family man,
grow old with one woman.
But the warrior bares thorny teeth

at domesticity, slurs in disgust
at the dreamer's naïveté,
and wants to brawl unafraid of dying young.

Tonight my infant is me
and I am her. I see myself
as I was born,
innocent and perfect, whole life ahead of me,
and I see she can become me,
no good. I hum, holding her tight,
melting into one hug, humming
until dawn thaws frost down window casements
into stucco cracks, stray hounds croon in ruts,
yeowling cold from jaws, tooth-scratching
stickers from paws, and I walk and walk,
my sleeping infant in my arms,
humming hurting-man blues.

Thinking how to give my family a better life,
I stroll the ditch bank next morning,
surprised to see pebbles last night's rain uncovered—blues
and greens. I want my tears to reveal
what is covered in me like that.
I throw a stone in the irrigation water;
where it gasps my child's awestruck mouth
glistens for breath, for a chance at life, glimmering ripples calling
me to be a real father.
I realize I must start today.
Where the stone hits is the center of the ripples,
where the stone hits is the center that causes action. Where
the stone hits is the beginning;
where I am now
is the center. I am the stone I held in my hand as a kid
and threw to see how far it could go.

Now, at twenty-one,
I pray

my lightning self
carved from thrown-away woodpile days
a faith
cut deep to the knot-core of my heart,
giving me a limb-top buoyancy,
an awakening, a realization that I am
a good man, a good human being,
healing emotional earthquakes in myself.

Twenty-eight

I will never be able to liberate myself satisfactorily
from the things I've done. Something in me, inconsolable, instinctive,
drives forth into the darkness of things. I wish to arrive at the
    circle of life
where darkness is my womb. I wish to give birth to a black rose, a
    jagged
silver flower stem, so heavy it lies like a Mayan pyramid in my hands.
With almost all things I do, I am left standing asking, How did I
    do it?
Beyond my life a darkness descends, a soft darkness that whispers
    to me to rest.
To rest in the wild outlying uncivilized land of myself, unpre-
    pared, humble,
I give myself to the unknowing. My plans are made of moments.
Like so many cells moving under a microscope,
my life under police and government surveillance
has left observers wondering on the miracle.
            For all the suffering and hardships,
for all the free-giving moments of laughter between,
I want to thank the Great Maker of All Things.

Twenty-nine

Thinking back:
Andrew at my side saying, "Leo's dead.
If we don't stop, man, there's nothing in it."
And I look down at his fingers, flamenco fingers,
twisted like piñon branches,
brittle with thirst—

> too much soul sun
> too much sand
> too much wind

in Andrew's life.
Looking over our lives, we see endless scrub-desert land
and not a person coming our way.
While we drive to Santa Fe
his world is in the heroin grain.
He looks at me and asks, "Why?"
Haggard man, purple under his eyes from insomnia,
and in the crook of his arms
black tracks where needles have sucked blood—
fanged needles of glass bats
we the vampires have given our lives to.
"Play your music, Andrew," I say,
looking straight ahead through the windshield.
"Living behind your mother's house in a shack,
play your death song on your guitar."

I was hitting four grams a day,
crystallizing my brain like a glass quartz,
my veins iced solid—
my voice the sound of cracking limbs—
buried under the snow
the man I was,
frozen with cocaine snow on my mustache,
the white dust covering my jacket, my black hair,

my eyelids; my mouth open, my eyes cold and brown,
staring off into space.

Now I've been clean
and my soul's in a spring of its own
and my words thrust up through the melting frost
like field flowers.
I'm starting again to be human, to feel my heart
pump sap through this old tree-body
hatchet-marked, chainsawed, lightning-struck,
the knife-sharp cocaine crystals,
the buzz,
the black smell of myself burning,
through the gashes, the black splotches, the blood pouring,
small green buds unfold like baby hands
to the new spring.

Thirty

The day I stopped
being an alien to myself was that afternoon
meeting Benny at Cuco's café,
a familiar restaurant with Mexican soft drinks,
laborers with hip-hung dirt-grimed jeans
and faces beaten by sun and wind
to look like real human faces.
Ordering a Coke, sipping it at the table,
I knew it was the last time I'd booze it up, get high,
knew the world around me was caving in,
saw two men on Coors fighting, saw one get shot,
the fights on the basketball court,
my own sweetness assaulted, my new change
unable to bear the sight of my old selves.

I stopped at a corner and saw a retarded woman
and her boyfriend fighting, her weeping and trying
to slice her wrist with their apartment key,
he pacing red-faced, beside himself, not knowing
how to appease her
as she sat on the bus bench whacking at her wrist,
and later this guy on the freeway honking his horn
with no one around, laying his hand on it,
blasting away out of sheer insanity.
Me seeing all this, worried about bills,
about confessing to my lies, deceptions,
feeling sensitive and morally healthy as I never had,
knowing the time for reckoning had come,
how I had to tell it all, cleanse myself,
because in all other areas I already had been
preparing for my long-awaited freedom, waiting for it,
how it clawed at me where I tried to hide,
sniffed me out hungrily, demolished barricades,
the walls I'd constructed, seeing how parallel
lives I'd lived streamed around me, seeing myself
in that retarded girl, the prisoner in the back of the cop's car,
the guy madly honking his horn—too many
hotels drunk and high with women I didn't know,
too much violence, too many
breakdowns and too much pretended happiness,
all those nights lying in the dark
huddled up, waiting for the torturous racks of pain
to subside, waiting to be sober, to be clean, to be true—
sheets drenched in sweat, face drawn and haggard,
eyes weak and humbled—thinking how it happened again,
how again I'd fallen, again I'd been ensnared,
my soul filled with evil.
I remember the last day
when I ingested drugs, how the chilling filled
my veins, my heart, with corruption, venom,
how after all the work I'd done to stay clean
I'd become a sordid clown,

how that day, that very Sunday afternoon,
could be, would be, must be
the day I stopped.

Thirty-one

Back in night school
to get my GED—
15 mph
I leave the school's welcome sign
behind, then steer
downslope, tires sizzling gravel,
to a stop sign.
Pass a blackened factory building,
slow down and turn right
through residential blocks,
barbered lawns, and living room lights
until I come to rooms for rest
with two dump trucks parked out back.

Pass 7–Eleven and on the green,
step it up and leave
35 mph behind, flick brights on
speed sign full of bullet holes,
up to 60 on a curving country road.

In my rearview towns glow,
bugs zing in headlight nets,
earth smells rush through air vents,
mailboxes are tin mules' back ends
grazing fenceless yards, ponds and woods,
tobacco fields and rusty barns,

deer crossing signs and red eyes wing
in my headlight's tunnel while frogs
rigid-rigid-rigid-rigid
and my windshield fogs, my arm on the car door,
a big truck smacks with a gush of air and roar.

At the yellow BEER sign of Mr. Hendron's country store
I turn right down a few fields
and then left into my weedy dirt driveway.

On a chair under the big oak tree
Riffy says, "How's she going?"
"Night school's a bitch," I say,
as he hands me a bag of fresh-picked tomatoes
from his field and then the bottle.
I swig, and say, "Moon's howling tonight."
"Be coming a rain," he says.

Thirty-two

On the doghouse,
clutch bathroom vent pipe
and pull myself onto flat roof
       of my adobe house.
Hoist a hand ax, bucket of tar, and trowel
with a rope tied to a belt loop
on my jeans.

The cottonwood branch
cracked through the radiant ashes
of my dream last night, still warm
on my pillow as I dashed

into the kids' room
thinking bunk beds had collapsed.
They were asleep.

Barefoot in boots,
in my bathrobe I swept
the snow-smoking limbs.
Wind complained
like a captive,
begging mercy, mercy.

I found the snap—an immense jaguar
of busted bark,
drooled September sap,
and growled fresh timber fangs.

I tarred the clawed stucco,
then raked the seasonal scum molt
of years' fur,
and tossed the leaves and twigs down on the ground.

Beto's mean machine
hummed—I slid down
the vent pipe, leaped one-footed
off the doghouse, grabbed my bag, cooler, thermos,
kissed my wife and kids,
                and met him in the driveway,
my life vibrating
with the ritual torch
of a new beginning,
bright on every tree and field we pass
                on my way to work.

Thirteen Mexicans

One

      Celebrate how Europeans stepped off every wood line,
         sea line, mountain ridge, and valley line and fenced
         them as their own
      celebrate how Los Indios waved with children in their arms
and how the captain shot them
      celebrate the treaty of peace Europeans signed
only to rise at midnight and slaughter the sleeping warriors
      celebrate how pioneers stripped thousand-year-old forests
to build Philadelphia and Boston
how they excluded Indios from fishing the streams
and how water flowed into slave plantations
and fields of the wealthy.
      Celebrate how Columbus wondered at the clean waters
         and air and fowl
and animals their hungers would feast on
      celebrate the land subdivided for exclusive estates
and how millions of human beings became landless and infected
    and were slaughtered
how centuries of deep coexistence with Mother Earth
was scoffed at and smudged out in the ashes and bullets and
    swords of Europeans
      let us celebrate the town meetings to hang Indios
      let us celebrate the political decisions to exile Indios from
         Turtle Island
      let us celebrate Columbus's arrival and how all the Holy
         Names were changed to accommodate the thick ox
         tongue of muttering English and Spanish ones
      let us celebrate how all the paintings depicted Indios as

savages killing and drinking the blood of blond-haired
children
celebrate the development of banks on hunting grounds
and carriages gilded and silked bearing pompous Englishmen
through crisp streets and Spanish women wearing safari jackets,
setting up their easels beside fishing streams
to paint their Georgetown mansions
celebrate how death was entertainment and
holy relics of feathers and drums and talismans became table
decor and circus spectacles
celebrate chained and guarded houses for open meadow
tepees
celebrate the beaver gloves and hats
performance stables with horses with braided manes
and Indio scalps and skin nailed to barn rafters
celebrate the unspeakable crimes of lawyers
drafting laws to rob ancestral lands
celebrate all their accountants sore-eyed at midnight
under reading lamps tirelessly counting endless stacks of criminal
money
celebrate the landscaped European gardens
God in every bush an Indio pruned
God in every glint of sterling dinnerware an Indio polished
God in every sheet an Indio washed
celebrate the spirit broken and the body abused beyond
recognition
let *si señor* slurp off our tongues to the patronizing bullshit
let us smile at the pitying glances
let us celebrate the rape of our women
let us be devoured by their contempt
let us saintfully give ourselves to the mob to be burned
and hanged
let us wear yokes around our necks
let us parade all the imprisoned and drive carts heaped
with all the dead
birds through Washington

let us compose elaborate symphonies and marching bands
    through Virginia's tobacco fields with thousands of slaves
let us stand at the shores of every ocean and lake and stream
and sing the glory of killing and murder beyond comprehension.
    Come, let us celebrate the churches that accused us of
        being devils
    celebrate the burning of our sweat lodges and eagle and
        herbal medicines
    celebrate all the lies in books how we were heathens
        with no songs
or culture
    celebrate the empty mountains and valleys
    celebrate how the once hip-high grass of the plains
is now ankle-high crusty scrub owned by millionaire cattlemen
    celebrate that America has not acknowledged the terrible
        crimes
of having done what we accuse it of
    celebrate the pardon of white-collar thieves and murderers
        by presidents,
not by society, God, or me
    celebrate the devastating willful tragedy
    the willfulness of racists decrying no racism
    the willfulness of torturers decrying no violence
    the willfulness of supporters of the Quincentennial
    decrying it was all roses and blessings. . . .

    Let us celebrate the frontier adventurer
marauding Mexican families and taking their homes
    celebrate the courageous Daniel Boone trapper
purposely betraying and lying
    celebrate the gluttons who triumphed
through treachery and murder in broad daylight, destroying all
    who were different
    celebrate the portrayals of God's chosen people
as a people who never harmed an ant
    celebrate in Santa Fe the pure-blood Spanish romantic idea
that they were heroes

celebrate the madness of historical oppression in
San Antonio
with reigning queens and mariachi music and mayoral speeches
celebrate in Los Angeles the agony of millions
with confetti and whoopla fanfare and awards to Hispanics
with foundations giving millions to create parades in hundreds of
cities
let us celebrate our own death and oppression
let us take solemn vows that nothing bad ever happened
that Columbus brought only enlightenment and baptized us
and we became God's innocent children
let us believe there was no sorrow
let us commemorate the hate and contempt they brought
for us
let us celebrate their scorn
let us celebrate this play written in grants and announced
in every city
how they loved us and let us live peacefully on our lands
how act after act and scene after scene
depicts them sharing their food and songs with us
how not one of us ever has encountered their vengeance
how Columbus brought in scene 1 flowers and love from
Europe
how scene 2 tells how his men humbled themselves in
our homes
and respected us
how scene 3 shows pure friendship and no hate or fear
portrays how they cared for us and how life was filled with joy
let us celebrate this with despair in our hearts
and blindfolds over our eyes
celebrate the denial of Indio slaves to the highest bidder
celebrate how we were leered at and spit at in every town
celebrate how we starved and how our children became
silent
celebrate our infant mortality rate and alcoholism and
drug addiction

celebrate the despair and unremitting depression of our
     people
celebrate how everyone agrees with everyone
celebrate how we grieve
and celebrate each sharp sword tip stained with our blood
celebrate each pencil and ink quill filled with lies
     celebrate doors closed to us from fear
and celebrate the glassy blue eyes that stare at us
celebrate each dagger that plunged into trusting brothers'
     and sisters' hearts
     celebrate the false piety and false modesty of investors
who thrive on our sadness and love
     celebrate this long bloody genocide with bottles of
Coors beer and Gallo wines
and quench the thirsty throats of racketeers
so they may have strength to fill every American street dancing
     over our bones.

     Let us celebrate the Quincentennial of Columbus's arrival
and not taste the bitterness
not recognize their insatiable appetite for more blood, more land,
     more money, more power.
     Let us rise in every quarter of the country on platforms
and give testimonials on how we must hate ourselves
and how we must teach our children to be ashamed of their past
     let us teach ourselves to forget our drums and songs
and stand in every classroom to praise the Star-Spangled Banner
     let us kiss bullets that bring peace to us
     let us love our poverty and be fearful of speaking our
          native language
in public
     let us bear our pain in silence and bow before the perpetrators
     let us call rabble-rousers those who dare to speak up
     let us turn our heads from each other and try to be white
          Americans
     let us kill each other drunkenly and drip with blood

let us give our homes to banks and bail bondsmen
let us christen ourselves and humbly accept our rulers'
    divine law
let us pray we remain cowards with no honor
let us forget this poem and walk out tonight
leaving our children without father or mother or home or history
  or culture
        and celebrate Columbus's arrival.

Two

Why not erect a statue of a mestizo Chicano poet
who doesn't deny his Spanish or Native American ancestry
but builds on both? Let there be poems
of Tonantzin, Great Mother Earth,
        celebrating how they've nurtured us, cared for us,
        loved us, and keep mothering us
        with their great blessings.
Get this guy on his horse
        the hell out of here,
        bolt the statue down in front
        of national Viagra headquarters
        where the hard-on is all that counts,
        or maybe he can be a mascot
        for WWF,
        World Wrestling Federation,
because if you want recommendations
for people who've honored
both Spanish and Indio spirits,
try Pablo Neruda; the villagers at Analco,
the first mestizo village;
try Jimenez, Lorca, or Hernandez.
                    *   *   *

Bring those who've given their hearts
        to the people out in public,
        instead of this conquistador
        rampaging through Burque—
        shortly put, my brothers and sisters,
        find a hero that symbolizes
        peace and compassion and unity among us
                not some metal-encased power-mongering
                hustler who didn't get his way
                and, pouting, started cutting off hands and feet
                because the brat couldn't always win the game.

Well, the rules have changed
for all your suited/skirted purebloods on both sides.
It's time to get real and realize
        Mother Earth and La Virgen de Guadalupe,
        the sun, the moon, the mountains,
        the water, the winds, the air, our elders,
        our mothers and fathers, our children,
        are the true explorers,
        the true discoverers,
        the true heroes and heroines.
                Got it?

Three

Driving home last night, I thought about
the lecture from a famous poet in Utah—writing poems for
    language only,
splicing the hot wires of language, to reconnect them
for more wattage to run the poem. The booklet I picked up at
    the desk,
written by an esteemed academic, gave praise to these poets,

set on stripping the word like a broken-down computer,
programming the poem until it was pale, bland erudite language
used only by a chosen few.
I don't understand this type of poem,
ticker-tape verbiage celebrating one poet's achievement
in rounding the cape of verb, claiming a new discovered land,
pillaging and ransacking the meanings,
until the victor poet rides through the university hallways.

Poetry goes much deeper than this. In the dark of the freeway,
in my beat-up Volkswagen, I think words
are important to a poor man, who has to survive in other ways
than studying from 8 A.M. to 6 P.M.
in the cozy corner of a library. Words for me rise
like the pope's hands on Easter Sunday. They carry
importance, like the first pink rose blossom that unfolds
after the winter. Each word has a wound in it,
the nail wound of someone hammering it up
on their own cross of meaning. I try to relive the making
of the wound, relive what made the word cry out
in pain, the scene, the voice that spoke it,
and I gradually take the word back
to a place when it could make miracles happen,
and here in my small cold office, it rises from the dead
tomb of academic text, naked,
and I clothe it, as it walks out into the world
to feed the hungry
with the meaning of a small brown sparrow on a branch.

Four

So many loose ends I feel like a kitten caught in a yarn shop with all the shelves toppling and balls of yarn entangling my limbs inextricably.

About race. I have various stances on that. First, you're talking to a homeboy who grew up in institutions most of his life. In my village there were no black folks. In the orphanage I met Allen Flood, a cool dude who tightened up as buddy with us. Later, however, after the orphanage, I happened on him in the same 'hood and he was a stone cold junkie. Didn't matter though, we loved him. What little balogna and Rainbow bread we had we shared with him, Spam and welfare cheese blocks too. Then he went to prison and vanished from the landscape.

I went to Lincoln. The majority of the students were black, and us Chicanos and them blacks fought all the time. We were like pit bulls straining at the chains to get at each other and for no other reason than we were bored and enjoyed the clashes. They were blood rituals for poor boys growing up. Try to kill each other off, like the colonist inculcated in us. Save them custard eaters (it's what Indios called the white man) the effort of getting off their porch rockers—we did it ourselves to each other: our ghetto-barrio teatime hour.

Undertakers, car-parts stores, drive-up liquor windows, dealers, and drive-bys dominate the barrio. Cemeteries and funeral homes languish in luxurious shade trees and gleaming limos and we all dream one day of homesteading on a grave or vacuuming gut out of corpses for the thrill of riding in a limo.

Somewhere in the chaos, roaming the streets, Quincy became my friend and he took me home. His father Otis let me live in the house. I fell in love with Quincy's sisters, curved and sensuous, bathing in a big washtub in the living room, I left the room when they bathed. Nighttime I became the best damn chicken rustler this side of the Rio Grande.

Jail and prison fostered horrible racism. I never indulged, in fact, and on numerous occasions broke up fights because blacks and whites were my friends and I ended up doing thirty in the hole, if you dig that.

Whites wouldn't hang with blacks and blacks kept away from whites. Taboo voodoo.

I had some gorgeous black women as girlfriends. I regret I had to move on. In South Carolina I got jumped by a bunch of ax-wielding crackers because I was with my babe. Other times KKK threw some ass-wipe rag of a newsletter in my yard predicting my demise. I could, however, shoot for the whites of eyes as good as any bowlegged Kentucky hick and I wasn't too bothered by the milk-jug white-liquor-toting intimidation.

I pain more at the Appalachia twang of a rusty violin string than the white-knuckled trigger click.

I grew up in the midst of socially sanctioned racism, brute, bloody, blade-dripping, barrel-smoking racism. In the twenties, wanna-be yahoo cowboys roped and strung up my people from Wyoming to Chihuahua. The dawn was pretzled with snapped necks and lifeless limbs.

While scholars and academics from prestigious universities write endless volumes about the slavery days, I wonder why they overlook the slavery prevalent today with my people. Millions of us survive in cardboard shacks in squalid camps without drinking water or even the most basic human facilities. No school. No medicine. We're paid a buck an hour. We're chased off the field before we get paid. We die from pesticide poisoning. We drink ourselves to death. We screech and gasp and die from sunstroke.

Babies are born with two fingers, no spine, two heads, and the growers and agricultural monsters spend millions on political games to scam as much as they can from us.

And I wonder why on the one-hour black TV shows where the pundits levy their grave opinions on the state of the nation, when they spew blustery brain-breakers, when Washington panels are chaired by only blacks, what the fuck happened to us? Why should the blacks speak just for themselves and be considered the only minority living in America? Shit, before any black stepped foot on the beach we'd been here hundreds of years.

What the fuck's that trip about?

What's with the black/white issue?

Why were we warehoused with the barest nod to civil rights; why weren't we even given water for the infants; why didn't any news reporter look around; why do personality wizards on TV accept the secondhand opinion of blacks speaking for us, when those blacks have never stepped into a Chicano's house and broken tortilla?

Why, if I am as native to this land as the minerals in the soil, do I still not exist? Why am I invisible? Why am I looked upon as a threat? Why do people see me as lazy when I die working, when my ancestors were slaughtered and genocide was the tune of the times, why can't I speak my language without duress from others, why must my culture be reduced to sombreros and castanets, why must I be stopped and checked for a citizenship card when I should be asking others? Why must I despair and fall prey to doomsday depression and be sucked up by drugs and whiskey and die in the gutter mumbling in my own language a prayer to Tonantzin, the earth goddess.

That's why there are angels; they help me carry the load of such oppressive doings.

That's why there are prayers; I pray a lot.

Seems every time a good man comes by, you hold out a biscuit-bill and that good man prances like some crystal-headed poodle on two hind legs dancing on the Jay Leno show to the applause of people who don't give a smelly billy goat's ass where this country goes; as long as they can turn the Wheel of Fortune, man, heaven has been attained.

I deplore racism. I don't even know what the word means. I know what pain is, what death is, what a beating is at the hands of goon squads with lead-filled batons whacking bones, but the word *racism* is almost a joke these days. People wearing Gucci shoes speak about walking barefoot over glass shards and hot coals; the closest they've come to experiencing bowel-singed and battery-cabled testicles and split faces and broken arms is glancing at the calendar dates that commemorate Martin Luther King's march to Selma.

That's like the billionaire lady who gives a fruit basket once a year at Christmas to fulfill her obligation to the starving children.

I don't know what racism is.

I know what it feels like, how it burns, how it bleeds, how it cries, how it lies sleepless night after night, how it cannot pay bills, how it cannot go to good schools, how it sleeps under project stair-wells, how it sells drugs to alleviate the hopeless, how it manipulates brother against brother and sister against sister, how it burns justice with the yard weeds, how it scoffs at poverty, how it fucks the Statue of Liberty, who lifts her dress for every racist entering the country and gives it up, ass and all. I know that racism.

But not the racism these suckers chitchat over on TV Sunday morning. Not the racism that some assimilated lobotomized puppets mimic in newspaper columns but the racism that steals life and breath from children, that bludgeons the man stooping in row fields, that rapes the mother's dream and breeds nightmare maggots in the virgin's womb.

Racism ferments in the fat man who lives on Mommy's money, in the fat man who desires to destroy all who disagree with him, in the fat man who backslaps and guffaws at a table with black folks and then later brags to others how he so thoroughly and sincerely understands the plight of the disadvantaged. In the fat man whose money is the ticket for his entry into people's graces, racism ferments in his gully gut like tadpoles in a stale pool of drainage water and infects our digestive tracts.

Where racism thrives you will find no men, none who have lived life, who have earned their money, who sleep well. Racism is nourished on fear, wrapped in unassuming good-natured birthday bow-tie philanthropy, creased with jowly good-fella smiles. It cools our rage at our cancerous failures like a bleak nuclear wind; it appears at the courthouse, the jail, the counselor's office, and the teacher's room cloaked in Samaritan goodwill, exhaling its toxic evil into our nostrils.

We succumb to it, turn on our own and accept, appeal to the racists, and get that nice juicy kissable paycheck that not only pays bills but doubles as a weapon against those who are not racists.

Conversion is business as usual. Get one spoiled apple in a barrel and in time others get the rot, blemish, bruise; the pulp of character oozes venomous sap that WASPS find savory.

I have a lot of fine white people I love; I know browns and blacks and Indians who preach virulent racism. Racism is about

privilege, undeserved and unearned authority, tyrannical power,
wealth amassed corruptly, sniveling lace-handkerchief judges smack-
ing their parched lips, impatiently clocking the minutes before they
can leave for the country-club cocktail hour.

Five

Wind chill factor 11 below. All night
wind has been fighting bare-chested trees
like a West Texas tent evangelist
hissing sin . . . sin . . . sin . . .
fist-cuffing nail-loose
tin
that intercoms between gates clanking
in the courtyard
and horses neighing in a field.

> Storm-wrecked black ships
> of clouds drift in
> from the South
> and crush their hulls on rooftops.
Tonight the atmosphere is thick with dread.
Tonight our fact-file lives
topple like statuary fragments.

A few miles north of here,
beyond the Juarez–El Paso border
nightscopes pick up human heat
that greens the fuzz helicopter
dash panels.

> A mother whispers,
> "*Shh, mejito, nomas poco mas alla.*"

Dunes of playing dead people
jackrabbit under strobe lights
and the cutting whack/blades,
                    "*Shh, mejito*," to her child
                    staggering in blinding dust
                    and gnashing wind.
Those who are not caught
will scratch sand up
and sleep against the warm
underbellies
of roots and stones.

There is a fog that rolls over,
obscuring the easy path to take.
I am on a pathless course—
my thoughts, feelings, dreams,
at any given time
are glass chimes in the wind.

How I hate border towns!
Cloaked men in doorways
raffle off children to bidders
from Los Angeles and Miami:
the smells of sewage and tropical mildew,
the cries of fruit-cart vendors,
the traffic shrieks.

There is a building where refugees sleep.
Three-story structure, fronted with decaying columns
and fluted mold. Hundreds of refugees
peek out from blankets, suspicious. I step over
rolled-up sleeping men, coughing children,
women nursing babes. Room after room
is filled with sickly, thin people. I think
of wounded soldiers back from the front. The people
catch stagnant water dripping from ceiling pipes
in their mouths. The children pick and eat

chipped stucco from walls, their fingers scabbed
from scratching off their meals. Coyotes
come to lead groups across the border. Others
wait their turn, building a fire from street scraps.
In the flame's fringe, their faces are gray and ashen.

They weave tales of horror
               in Guatemala
               Dominican Republic
               Uruguay
               Brazil
               Puerto Rico
               Argentina
               America
               and Mexico.
Their language is filled
with words of
               Intelligence Center
               Customs Service
               Death Squads
               Immigration and Naturalization
               Courts
               Prisons.

At suppertime
my daughter and wife
bring them pots
of cabbage and beans.

I hear their stories and we are no different.
They tell of clumps of snow on field posts,
how ice furs the rumps of horses,
how they themselves once exhaled
the vigorous icy air of mountains, long ago,
in another world, when the full moon rose
above pine trees and lit their faces,
as the flames do now.

Six

I know little about the ferocious fire
and ocean heft of steel and molten red masses
that blisters and ashens the air
calluses the hands and burns one's cheeks
and I know even less
   how steel is molded and prefabbed
   cools and hardens
   or how it is transported
      by sixteen-wheel Macks
      hoisted by cranes and bolted down
      to create cities
      bridges
      buildings
      streetlights.
All of this is a mystery—
but there is something very human
and suffused with the splendor
of the human soul
when I think how delicate
tiny screws and wheels for watch workings
and tonnage of tank armor
and how so much of the world is clad in steel
from computer fibers
to satellites orbiting the earth.
But what I want to say—
trying to get at the miracle
of a steelworker's heart—
is how days have been so hard
that his tears have fallen
like molten steel-bead shavings from a welder's torch,
how he's carried his family through rough times
like a bridge kept intact during an earthquake,
how there's something that smells and tastes like steel
in his heart,

this connection
to earth matter
to mined minerals
is the ancient occupation
practiced thousands of years ago
by those who hammered plowshares and swords,
horseshoes and coins,
taming the metal
        silvering our bodies with ornaments
        to the stature of gods
        with steel that endures freezing and fire,
        wrenched from ice and granite
        and processed into a pickup or fork—
and few occupations can claim
engagement with such a mythical mineral
that we might thrive
in the seasons of a lifetime.

Seven

The ticket was paid
to the life I enjoy
by the many relations who came before me:
sheepherders, miners, steelworkers, field-workers,
carpenters, ranchers, janitors, maids—
        commonsense folks,
        devout Catholics,
        dressed and washed and working at sunrise
        quitting when they could no longer see their hands
around the shovel handle, each
with a dream nourished
with laughter, raked soil soft around the roots,
until the next generation cut a branch

and made a bow and arrow,
    the next made shoes and baskets of its bark,
    chiseled and scraped saplings to fiber for rope,
made canoes, knives, kept the fire lit,
shared songs and stories,
    ignored calluses, aches, wounds,
    believed in light as a god, spring as a woman,
    rarely had money,
kept food on the woodstove simmering for hungry visitors,
kept their word,
kept their clothes mended and wore them
until blue cloth turned white and shiny buttons glossed dull,
tool handles grooved with grip:
Mexicans and Native Americans,
every day carrying their lunch box to work,
ensured one day I'd have a book to read,
I'd be free to walk down a street
without police harassment,
without being prosecuted for the color of my skin
or my culture,
not be mocked or ridiculed,
all paid for by my relations
before me,
    riding pickup beds to the fields,
    sweating with a short hoe in the rows,
dreaming one day their children's children,
the ones who did not die prematurely at birth
or from slave work,
would have freedom to express their beauty.

Eight

When Father's ring
was passed down to me, I slipped it over my finger—
turquoise stone bordered by silver.

I was now conscious of my hand. At stoplights,
or waiting for a friend in a café, or off writing by
myself, I studied the landscape of the ring:

> The center of the stone ridged with an arroyo,
> and white waving lines as if autumn geese
> flew in the blue stone.

I thought of the turquoise mines near Magdalena,
and the squat bronzed-face Apache Mejicano miner
who picked the stone. And the mountain that had formed
the stone into a blue raindrop
> during the rains of universal beginning,
> when all things were given faces and voices,
> shaping the ring
> into an epic:
clanks of iron cars' wheels, picks and shovels
clanged against rocks, I heard
hidden within the stone
passed down generation
> to generation.

Nine

Maria's husband
    vanished from the face of the earth.
How would you feel
if you woke up and your family was gone,
never a letter, a call,
and no matter who you asked, they would blush with timidity,
    frightened,
           that a human being
               can vanish
                   into nothing.
Where are the graves?
Or do they employ
body-shredding machines, and toss mashed bone and flesh
into the sea?

Outside your house now
snow and ice break branches
that dangle from electric lines.
If the line broke,
    if the city disappeared,
        if all people were gone
            from the face of the earth
            when you woke up,
how would you feel?

How does it feel for a man
to be alone
inside a torture chamber,
knowing within hours he will die and never
say goodbye to wife and children?
These are people who speak the same language I do,
who have children I have,
who work the earth as I do,

who enjoy the pleasure of making love
and biting into an apple.

No books to explain such cruelty,
no words to speak the unspeakable
silence that fills me with
horror.

I feel a cold from all the unexplained deaths,
all the Disappeared.
Their silence grows and grows
as the stack of bones buried in secret graves
bullets worm.

Here each mother's womb
is a rock carried beneath the belly,
and each man's eye a damp cellar
where thieves sleep.
Each tongue is a bleeding stub.
Each finger on a trigger
is a coffin nail,
as the black hearse of grief
drives into each breast.

Ten

Having a family changes things.
Years ago in Taos, Andre from Transylvania
via New Orleans
boasted he could outdrink me
and we bought a quart of vodka for him,
mescal for me; then we went to the local

radio station for an interview:
halfway through on air
he drooled saliva and bubbled on the mike,
whispering could I score some weed
or something to sober him up—
and in Chicano slang
so our host could not understand
I announced if anyone listening had weed
coke or buttons
to meet us in the parking lot;
afterward
poetry lovers greeted us
offering booze and drugs, and
with an impromptu tailgate and on Chevy hoods
we partied
clinked bottles, swigged, and chugged
until someone shouldered Andre away
limp as an empty gunnysack
and I saluted his courage by toasting
from his half-finished bottle
my victory.

      Having a family changed all that—
I can't party like I used to.
I take Marisol to her Little League games, the batting cage
where she smacks over a hundred pitches,
        take my daily vitamins
        blend fruits for a smoothie,
        garlic and fiber every meal,
        I run five miles a day, swim, bicycle, and shoot pool,
        pay auto insurance and mortgage—
but while I run
I wooze into reveries
when during Mother's Day in Santa Fe
I was invited to read
and the old ones to the left were chattering away,
middle-aged men in the center of the square

discussing racehorses, and the young to my right
were flirting and giggling and applying mascara,
when all of a sudden I cried out *Muthafuckas!*
and every able-bodied man in the crowd
came after me. I whispered to Laura,
Get the car and pull it around in back, quick!
and just before they leaped onstage
to pummel us with tortilla rollers, Victorio and I
leaped through the Volvo windows and sped away;
cans and rocks and sticks flying at our car,
we escaped to recite another poem.

      But having a family changes things:
you risk less and spontaneity is replaced
with planning.
No longer does all my money go on a single poker hand
in a Dallas hotel room—
and to sweeten the deal I toss in the truck title—
nor do I stay up as I did for weeks with friends
drinking Chinaco tequila and *sotol*
with bandits and outlaws on the run from ATS and FBI,
nor do I puke in the mayor's lap when he's talking about how he
understands poetry,
nor whiz the cylinder on a .45,
click the trigger back playing who's chicken,

      Having a family changes all that.
I enjoy waking early to greet the sun and recite my prayers
and give thanks for being alive.
I drive my older girl to Sandia Peak
for an all-day grueling 16.5-mile race up the mountain and back down
cheerleading her
absolutely ecstatic when she places fourth among three hundred
   competitors,
sweaty, exhausted, mud-grogged, almost passing out
she wavers across the finish-line banner,
where I bear-hug her, pat her back, and head to the grill

for burgers and lemonade:
such family joys high-water
foamy white-caps my journey
with island tides of innocence,
filling the trail of father's footprints in moist sand
with wild lashings of wave-laughters and tears
pains and joys of being the man they follow
not to get lost
as I got lost,
tempted by bad-boy wanderlust.
I smuggled guns across the border and sold them to bandits,
hijacked tractor-trailers loaded with freshly auctioned tobacco leaf
and sold it in Georgia,
           or sitting around King Louie's round table,
           days into weeks we snorted, smoked, and drank
           our dreams, turning into a moldy and dreary roadside
                carcass kill
           we carried on our backs,
scoffing at professors with their departmental sheaves
of bemused mouse droppings of poems.

Because we gypsies of the night didn't hold back,
we cried out poems,
gave birthing groans and spilled blood and wept and
roared with all the glory and fire of volcanoes
erupting and destroying villages,
leaving our own bones as fossils in the ash;
we grinned with contempt at literary corpses in cultural suits
whose domestic poems were tame as Halloween masks,
whose hands begged for attention
from soul-throttling English departments,
but around the table if such a poem dared be spoken
we'd drive the fraud out
as Jesus did the moneylenders from the temple;
we despised those who stole from others
calling it their own, trumped swollen frogs in the toxic pond
of their ambition,

they cackadoodle-do'd poems we knew were stolen
from street-corner poets or poets who had lent them
their manuscripts to read,
and paraded themselves with all the peacock fluff and pomp
of asses braying out the wrong end
after eating too many beans.
    But having a family
    rounds the sharp edge of your opinion
    and we listened to the stolen poetry
    and read the interviews acclaiming them
    the "greatest" or "masters" or "cultural godfather"
    and the rest of the cliché'd cud-spit,
    slimy alfalfa wads that drooled the pages
    of Sunday art sections.

    Having a family changes your temperament.
You become more tolerant
        of bad poems and poetry thieves and self-
            proclaimed "masters,"
        conscious more of bills
        than academic bile,
        more attentive to stool worms in dog shit
        than the book editor's parochial crap
        spoiling your first cup of morning coffee
        with his politically correct views,
        so pure and saintly
        it doesn't smell
        and you all know—
when you've changed enough diapers
you learn—
certain laws of nature just don't change.

    But having a family changes things.
I couldn't just pluck out of a hat
what direction I'd take or what I might do,
I had to be there for the crying and screaming and kisses and hugs,
revving poems on the page that could take the turns

I was taking;
no more bouncing on off-road trails across the prairie
for a shortcut to a place I was already days late in getting to;
no more lunches in avant-garde cafés in the Village
with a hundred different versions of lattes;
instead I spun spaghetti in the pot
so it wouldn't stick, and spooned
in sauce, and ladled out steaming heaps on plates.
Proud of small accomplishments,
like throwing a ball or swimming with my child,
achievements that have no rival
and need no plaque, banquet, or medal—
            having a family safe and healthy
            lets me sleep good at night,
            dream deep
            about new dishes I want to cook
            sure to keep salt and pepper shakers full
            have ample sugar and cereal.
            You learn the joys of gardening,
            smile when you enter the bathroom
            and see a book about magic tricks
            lying on the floor by the toilet,
            and while sitting in the Ferris-wheel chair,
            telling your daughter not to swing it,
            you see why you couldn't win a bear
            looking down at the basketball goal—
            it's oval—and decide to try
            the booth with the BB gun and paper red star—
            softballs tossed into the wicker fruit baskets
                wouldn't stay.
        These things matter when you have a family.

Eleven

So many times have I encouraged death into the arena of my day
to confront it proudly,
when my Harley veered in the rain at 80 miles an hour
and in front of me a stalled car welcomed my death,
when pistols were put to my head because I refused
to obey the policeman,
when thugs in Dallas armed with sawed-off shotguns
blasted away at me,
> these were but minor skirmishes
> compared to the day-to-day trials I face
> as a father, as a man committing myself to friends,
> sometimes wallowing in self-pity,
> sometimes fearful of getting out of bed,
> sometimes looking out on the world I feel such despair,
I thank You for allowing me to survive those moments
I think will never end.

> And I go on to praise the woman who continues
> her struggle to love life despite its horrid headlines,
> I praise the man who would be a racist and is not,
> the one who could cheat and decides to be fair,
> the one who opens his arms to you at the door
> and welcomes you in for a hot meal.
The open hearts of this miraculous land.
> they are the true poets and the true warriors,
> they are the ones whose hearts and souls
> keep this world safe from all innocence being destroyed,
and to all of you, there is a little boy
in my soul who has never given up dreaming for a better world,
and to you from his soft lips,
from his heart so entrenched in the eagle's flight
how he commemorates your common lives
with so much depth that all the violins in the world
tune themselves and all who own them

exit doors and can't you see them
in Italian cobblestone squares,
in New York lofts, Albuquerque barrios, and Oklahoma tribes,
in Idaho fields,
in Mexican villages, each note a beautiful voice, soft as Vermont
    maple syrup,
sweet as Whitney Houston's
singing, Blessed are you, blessed are you
who continue to believe in peace, in forgiveness, in hope,
blessed are your hands that offer help to the helpless,
your eyes that refuse to turn away from injustice,
your voices that continue to refuse to sell your heart,
your bodies that rise with aches and pains and exhaustion
to face yet another day on the journey that defines us as human
    beings.
Blessed are all of you:
        blessed is your path sprinkled with children's laughter
        and the elderly's whispers,
        even while your feet blister and your hands numb from work,
        your daily lives sing softly of illustrious joys.

Twelve

I walked through the garden this morning,
pleased that the roses were so bountiful, then spring,
in awe of the lilacs
        climbing over the wall,
                toward the sunlight, shivering
with freedom on the open road of light.
I don't remember my dreams.
I keep a journal next to my bed with empty pages
and an ink pen I haven't used yet.

This year dear friends of mine have died,
acquaintances I've admired
fellow poets I've honored as heroes and heroines,
who spent their heart's last sigh
their heels dug into the dirt against retreat,
their voices quiet comets of brilliant subversion
in the dark.
I've spent my days
            listening to the stark cries in the bone marrow
                of urban streets—
and I don't, as some poets do, slap their ass and grin
a toothy smile
flirting with the audience to lure their appeal
            with politically correct bullshit—
            I'm telling you,
                if you're going to read a poem about a kid getting
                    his head blown off,
                if you're going to raw-jaw your sugar tongue
                to gain favor and win the approval
of those who, unlike you, have never been
down on the streets, who have spent
their Sunday morning gleaning city papers
for topics to write about,
preach what you don't follow
who only visit the barrio and reservation
like tourists with concerned faces oohing and aahing
faked anguish over our misery.

            You should know
that poetry deserves more than a hee-hawing mule
bowing its head onstage to the roaring applause
            of an audience mad about appearance
            and ignoring the substance.
Whining what the crowd wants to hear,
recruit allies who succumb to your sheepish
poor-me poor-me victim maiden-in-distress,
look-what-they've-done suffering martyr in the burning pyre,

sit back and fuel the spectacle of mawkish compassion
from brittle-tempered, hollow-hearted New Age activists,
who fall at your feet on their knees and groan
            with livid rage
            how the world has done you wrong.
I'm telling you,
            the real world
            is where handouts don't come
            in the form of a thousand-dollar check
            from sympathetic patrons
            and airline tickets and classy hotels,
but bread to the starving hand,
freedom taken away for fifty years from a young man
or clubs beating down a Chicano kid in the street
            of which the only thing you've ever been taught
            or know about
            is that we
            can't be trusted,
            are thieves,
            drunks,
            addicts
            and illegal aliens—
Man, I am so tired of hearing this from frigid hearts
and castrated minds
            who have never engaged in life
            with their bodies and hands and blood and souls,
            that all I can ask you is
            Why do you get in the way when we got all this
                work to do?
Step aside, let us do the real work
            with our people,
            and you can have that soapbox on a corner
            and talk all you want.
Just stay out of our way;
we have work to do, step aside, please step aside.
It takes so much effort to go around you,
            as we follow tribal drumming god-beat boom

into the places where people die, suffer, hurt, are
desperate,
diseased, hungry, cold, shelterless.
We have work to do.

Thirteen

There is a place not far from here
I walk to on weekends: by myself sometimes,
sometimes taking my oldest daughter with me.
I point to the blueberry tree in the distance,
its two-hundred-year-old branches
clouding the sky green.

The long stand-thickets of grass loom over her head,
around my waist.
How the sun glows through the greed blades
like sunlight at dawn glows through my living room curtains.

Our boots sluck in the swampy ground.
Blue and red wildflowers
star the air.
Insects light as dandelion fluff glide over black standing pools.
In areas the cattails tower higher than my head.

No one ever comes here.
This place has been left alone for years,
settled like a raw jewel
at the foot of dormant volcanoes
the Isletas hold sacred.

I grip a handful of mud beneath the water
and bring it up. The earth is still forming,

I tell my daughter. We came from here, thousands of years ago,
this was known as the land of the Cranes,
and you and I are children of the Cranes.

We pause in silence listening to the humid whir
of grass leaning in wind,
cattails and tall grass softly crushing into each other.
I think back a moment to a time a few years ago,
when I was fishing at a pond in North Carolina.
Out of nowhere, on a standing dead tree overhanging the pond,
a crane swooped over the forest pines and landed on a branch.
It sat there staring at me,
white-feathered, long beak, still, like a small white cloud over the
    pond.
It seemed to say, Go back to your roots, now is the time.

Now . . . kneeling in the tall lush swamp greens,
I smell my birth here
and feel the fragments of who I am graft together
into this lean sharp wild grass,
and my soul bends with the wind
that rushes down the black mesa volcanoes,
into the grass.

Fourteen

Francisco has always worked the apple orchards
and melon fields,
he is what others call illegal alien,
or undocumented.

His father's fathers
crossed the borders

centuries before Columbus was born,
when borders were mythical lands
of different animals and plants,
when cold water in storm channels
was a water god, fins flashing.

Francisco smells the air
and knows when to head north. God calls.
He will sleep with his clothes on
so his children
can sleep under warm blankets.

Like a blazing meteorite
that rages into earth's atmosphere,
he passes *la frontera;*
vaporizing pride and language,
he becomes a dark mineral that cools down
in the Rio Grande.

By El Paso, children and teenagers
jump a culvert,
go through a hole in the cyclone fence,
tiptoe over beer cans, bedsprings, tires,
and drink the green water
bubbling chemicals out
of an industrial outpouring pipe.
They swim in the polluted foam.
And as Francisco's fingers numb
picking apples, he remembers
how he too drank from a spout once
and became sick. How he worked away
weeks of sickness
by sweating, working harder and sweating
until he had sweated it out.
It was the cure for everything. Work.

Fifteen

Now here in Colorado Springs, on this snowy Sunday morning, people enter churches in a town that is the national headquarters for more than thirty reborn frenzy-eyed religious battalions, armed with the moral conviction that they and only they are divinely blessed by God to dole out the rights and wrongs of human behavior.

Something happened to me when I could no longer support my family, when the bills continued at faster and faster pace to accumulate, when the rest of the world awoke on a Sunday morning like this and went to church in nice new clothes, when they later met at restaurants brimming with chattering successful types,

something happened to me when I was forced to raid cornfields only two weeks before I was offered this endowed chair, when my boys and I filled our paper grocery bags with corn and we ate corn for days, when I had to avoid the phone because collection agencies were hounding me every hour on the hour, when they cut off the lights and gas,

something happened to me when I walked into the Colorado State Prison and realized that nothing had changed in fifteen years; when I was in Phoenix to read and the news announced a man in prison was going to be fried in the chair

and meanwhile, something happened when the great poet and playwright Dancer died in a hospital after being raped in prison, living in the streets, and being addicted, when a Chicano named JB from Denver just the other day was pulled from his Denver public school bus by police and kicked and beat with flashlights and clubs and sixty children watched from the bus windows, the same JB who had the honor of going through the Sun Dance ritual and who was considered the bravest of all the participants, his flesh torn and body grueled by the intense agony of his prayers,

something happened when I was asked by America to write poetry that pleased the most selfish and arrogantly wealthy, and when I recited poetry roaring with contemptuous spite upon those who purchased justice and apathetic leisure, I was shunned by the academics and scratched off the foundation lists as someone who would receive no money from them,

because I spat in disgust at their Italian shoes and flicked my hand at their pretentious Armani suits, their flesh and bones no more human than the face and hands of an ordinary bedroom alarm clock,

something happened when their money meant nothing to me, when good clean young men and women out of unbearable despair and suffocating anxiety became addicts, when mothers were afraid to leave the county jail because life was better inside, when doctors and lawyers and school administrators refused medical care and quality education and justice because a person had no money, the ultimate foul and toxic rationale that contaminates our society and degrades all human beings who stand for what is decent and right,

something happened when I walked into a school in my barrio and the kids were reading history books about how one day we would land on the moon, and there was not a single computer for the whole school while uptown high schools had dozens, because of money,

something happened to me when for my entire life newscasts reported the news of ongoing wars between blacks and whites, Jews and Arabs, when Furhmans and Mansons and Nixons and Bushes and LAPDs and New Mexico police hit squads keep killing and maiming and beating and bludgeoning and raping and hating,

something happened to me when good water turned to poison from industrial toxic waste, when children were born retarded and deformed by corporate pollutants, when the most heinous of crimes by white-collar executives and companies were dealt with by a gentleman's handshake and a small fine equal to a lunch-counter charge,

something happened to me when my friend Emiliano, a gay priest, was so afraid of admitting it that he swam out to sea in San Francisco and never returned, when I walked with little black children in Camden, New Jersey, past block after block infested with boarded-up houses and street curbs buzzing with crack dealers, when the school was surrounded with barbwire and cameras and security patrols, when I visited the Camden prison and men of all colors wept and embraced when they realized what they had done to their lives and how they had let opportunity slip by, when they realized how terrible and sad their lives were,

something happened to me when thieves plundered Pablo Neruda's house after his death, when the great Chicano educational activist Cheyenne Segoya was assassinated for teaching George Jackson in the San Quentin barbershop about subversion and organization, when the Malcolm X movie dismissed the importance of the Puerto Ricans in prison who, being so religious themselves, threw their power and allied with the Muslims against the whites, allowing them to meet on the yard and teach men about spirituality and create Malcolm Xes,

something happened to me when poets who have nothing to write about are being published trumpeting a new movement when it's simply another mask to obscure their spiritual and emotional poverty,

something happened to me when Cisneros and Peña from the Clinton Administration went to South Central and groomed themselves for sound bites and photo sessions by appearing in the rubble and promising to help, while three days later in the park nearby thousands of RAZA families still had not been given emergency rations, not so much as a glass of water, when a black congresswoman from South Central rallied congressional support and international sympathy for blacks in the south central district, rejecting thousands of Latinos in the districts as foreigners and excusing the brutal atrocities against them, black vigilante gangs clubbing and beating innocent families and warehousing thousands of others without so much as an apology,

something happened to me, so don't ever ask why I do what I do and write what I write—
I just do it.

Something happened to me going through Bernalillo, a snowy frigid night, when after teaching writing and reading to Navajo kids in Farmington I stopped to refuel. I inched my window down and told this scraggly white kid to fill it up. After inserting the gas nozzle in the tank he kept staring and tapped my window. "Ain't you Mr. Baca?" I said yes and he continued. "You know, my girlfriend and I are fighting a lot and I keep this journal and I write in it every day, and if it wasn't for my journal, I don't know what I'd do, probably kill myself." I looked puzzled. "Don't you remember me? You came to my elementary class and taught us how to keep journals! Write poetry!" He smiled, a poor man's smile full of rich heart. I turned to my wife. "See, it works, poetry works, that's how it's supposed to work, not kept secluded like a pampered hermit in academia halls but out in the world, alive and working and pertinent to people and their lives!"

Another time at Kinko's I went in to copy a novel and the kid didn't charge me a cent: "You write good poems, there's no charge," and something happened to me when I went into the supermarket and old women came up to me and patted my shoulder saying I was doing a good job and the sackers, young sixteen-year-old bucks in high school with brown eyes and black hair, insisting that they carry my groceries out to the car, saying to me, "That movie you did is bad, really bad, and I went and bought your poetry after that—and man, I love poetry; I read it to my mom and sister and they like your stuff too,"

and it happened in alternative school where Joker had dropped out of school after fighting a few kids and stabbing two, and when I came to read, he was in the middle of a gang-banging drive-by turf war, crew-cut, tattooed, lean, wearing saggy bags and NBA Jordan tank top and Nikes, eighteen years old, and after I read the kids crowded me and yelled, "Yeah, Joker says you're his uncle, he's a low-life lying dog, says you his *tio*," and I looked at Joker standing three back in the crowd, his eyes large and wide as full moons, something in them wanting me to say yes, wanting someone in this world to claim him, wanting someone like me whose movie he saw and loved to claim him as family, and I reached my arms out and pulled him to me and hugged him, both of us crying, and me telling the class, "I *am* his uncle, I am," and me feeling Joker's fingers clawing deep into my bones and flesh, holding on me,

and something happened to me twenty years ago when I started the first homeless kids writing class in the barracks behind St. Ann's church and all my professional colleagues from the University of New Mexico mocked me as naive and romantic, saying

what I was doing was dumb and I was wasting my time, but I got
them to put their knives away and write poetry for a year and per-
form a play, and after twenty years it is still going,
            and I can multiply these stories a hundred times in as many
varieties, and I am still at it, while academic gossips on e-mail scrawl
absurd little assumptions about me, that I am a rough tough guy,
and wonder on the Net how my poetry ever got published and claim
it is not poetry, and fill their profound PhD and master of English
minds with ridiculous mongering rumors, and immerse their hearts
in the trough chatter peddling tasteless hearsay while the rest of us—
            just do it.

            Something happened to me when most of my friends opted
to die an early death,
            when the best of our poets wash their hands of society's
meowish morals and barking prattle,
            when they take up residence on the outskirts of the city and
choose to be poor and unpopular rather than have their time wasted
on critics,
            because they are writing poetry, busy with the business of liv-
ing up to standards that compel them to search the shadows of their
souls for light, to grace the abused child's hand with a caring hand,
offering hope to the hopeless in prison shattering the academic rooms
of mirroring lies with simple truths, following the traditions of true
poets as a reporter follows sirens to the scene of the accident, to where
people are in need of poetry, where people are hurt and need help,
            poets stalking beauty as a jaguar stalks a quetzal, its eyes
seeing better in the dark than in the daylight, scenting the air with
their tongues, picking up the slightest vibrations to learn where the
clumsy and arrogant intruder steps, out to kill it with a rifle,
            something happened to me to make me the way I am, and
how I live and what I say offers no excuse or apology—
            I just do it.

            Something happened to me when I saw the gorilla's eyes,
the eagle's constrained effort to spread its wings and fly, the pan-
ther laying up in its corner, and the horde of visitors to the zoo,

not that it is bad, but once in prison myself I felt for them, knew their hearts cracked like the pads of a sick dog dying thirstily for water and having none,

I felt the black hair of the gorilla cover my skin and its brooding eyes become mine, its black hands my own scratching at the concrete and knuckling away behind a rock to hide from the public gawkers because I did the same in prison; when visitors came by to view us, I turned my back on them,

and now as people exit churches and talk business deals over Sunday breakfast and ask about the kids and what schools they attend and how they are doing, now that athletic stores fill with bicyclists and weight lifters and health buffs, and stockers fill the vitamin shelves and others are thinking of buying treadmills and step climbers and ointments and creams for sore muscles, fishing gear, and bullets and camouflage for deer season,

poets walk at dawn to praise the sun and study the behavior of birds in the park and watch kids play soccer and basketball, and while church bells toll in the distance for the devout, poets pick leaves from the ground to place in the pages of their favorite books and wonder how to make a poem as beautiful and terrifying as reality is—poetry does not depend on the accouterments of convenience, it depends on the soul spinning like a leaf in the wind, a leaf with its underside red and its side facing the sun gold, a leaf unafraid of dying every year, unafraid of being torn from its roots, unafraid of turning brown and gray and pulverizing into tiny motes of dust to be scattered among the dung heaps of livestock to ferment and give nutrients to seedlings that will flourish with spring flowers and thorny evergreens.

We just do it.

Sixteen

Thirteen Mexicans,
each having paid from two fifty to five hundred
to the coyote to smuggle them in the United States to work,
crashed into the back end of a sixteen-wheeler
and died last night—
        the youngest thirteen.
They died wanting to work,
would have done anything for you—
washed your dirty clothes, dishes, scrubbed toilets—
        yet this morning no one thinks about them,
        no one cares who they were, what songs they had in their
            hearts,
        what their dreams were, who their parents were,
        just a bunch of wetbacks—
their blood, freezing on the highway pavement,
        reflects your indifference,
        marinates your food,
their disfigured, unrecognizable corpses,
        scattered heads and limbs and torsos
are remembered in the white-knuckle clenched fist I raise
to you
        who need your crops cut, fields hoed,
        houses cleaned, yards landscaped,
        children cared for—
thirteen of them last night,
        thousands more in growers' fields,
        restaurants,
        all-night gas stations
        and construction companies,
offered no medical care, no education, no sanitary living quarters;
dogs, cats, birds, and rats are treated kinder,
and no Georgia mule ever worked harder
than my Mexican brothers and sisters,
lacking citizenship papers but with heart, soul, and mind

full of dreams,
        worked and not paid, greeted when needed
but, after their work is finished,
crowded into cattle cars, truck beds, vans, jail cells, livestock pens,
shot, electrocuted, beaten, exiled, robbed, jeered at, blamed,
because they believe in the American Dream
we take for granted.
        Don't tell me slavery has ended,
        don't tell me there's no prejudice,
        or that judges rule fairly—
handcuffs, pepper Mace, cells, police, and the INS
were not created for the rich corporate executives.
Imagine having worked from dawn until dusk,
        then being cheated out of your pay,
        and when you get back to your freezing tent,
        the boss calls Immigration
        to drag you away so he doesn't have to pay?
Imagine your kids working all day in factory sweatshops,
        then being herded into paddy wagons
        and deposited on the border.
What hypocrisy,
        what a sham your prayers are at Sunday services,
        assuming you're more entitled to live and breathe and eat
        by exploiting the less fortunate.

Seventeen

These are the *madrecitas* we should bow before,
        reverently—
        they have never given up faith—
        bowed and gnarled legs, swollen ankles, puffy feet
        are Mayan jungle roots
        that awaken in me a reunion with grace.

I feel at peace knowing they live,
        prayers crumble from their mouths
        with the weight of humility and piety,
        hunched angels always in pain,
        joints swell with burning, knuckles,
        stark against the flesh, jut
        like ribs of a starved one sucking in a last breath.
These *madrecitas* have been used too long to help others.
        Their lives
        sonorous cathedral bells gong great
        iron -*ug* iron -*th* iron -*ug.*
Deserved blessing radiates from them,
        whose feet have hardened stone walks to burnished glows,
        puckered their wrinkled mouths to take the holy wafer,
        hummingbird beaks at honeysuckle blossoms.
Their residence on earth leaves flowers where they stepped,
        stooped all their lives in serving others,
and I watch them
        fold their feathered hands
        with impeccable grace and dignity
        and flutter around the cathedral steps
        gathering in the fruit of the altar,
        where candle flames are tawny peaches
        they hold in their hands and bite into
        like doves at dawn in the orchard.

Eighteen

I went with Rosetta
        to visit her newborn infant
        in the hospital nursery
        watching her don the maternity apron and white mask,
        then tickling and caressing her baby,

and after five minutes
giving her back to the nurses
        who informed her she couldn't take her child.

I ran after Rosetta and found her outside,
sitting behind the hospital building on the dirt, weeping.
        I sat with her on the dirt,
                skinny, disheveled, face smudged with makeup,
                her voice cringing words
                        pleading for her baby.
I said nothing, knowing she loved crack more.
Patients and doctors
had entered the emergency doors,
when this motherly Chicana woman, walking with her kids
to her car in the parking lot,
comes over, asking,
                "What's wrong sweetheart?"
The woman knelt down and combed Rosetta's hair with her
        fingers,
wiped her cheeks with her sleeve,
as Rosetta cried they wouldn't let her have her baby.
        "Now, now, now," the woman comforted her,
        "don't you worry, you'll have your baby."
"She's a crack addict," I said, "and she'll sell it for crack if she can."

The woman looked at me, and in her eyes, that instant,
I saw the infant a man twenty years from now,
in the dark,
traveling to cities, barrios, ghettos, reservations,
groping in his canvas shoulder bag
for poetry books to give out, poems to read, maps,
as his headlights spray past
        /red cliffs/,
                steel road bumper guards,
and he sees in the tall grass, foraging with claws and beak
a beautiful hawk,
that inspires him to be as real

in his poetry,
to come away with truth like a field mouse
dangling from his beak.
        "We'll get her into treatment then," the woman said,
      "and in the meantime we'll find a place for the baby."
          I jumped up and said, "Let's go."

Nineteen

Mother Teresa,
in the whorls of her fingertips
star-forming God's breath ignites
light
in the pores and blood of those
she touches.

Her hands give blessings to the world
the way a lilac does its fragrance
and grass blades their green.

At Lori's house in Wisconsin,
we peer into the foliage
weaving the north side of the wall,
pushing aside the tapestry of vine braidings
to look inside the robin's nest for an egg,
concealed from sight.
        "I've seen her
          but she hasn't come back in a while," Lori says.

The mantle of mutinous leaves and stems
is a braid. Spring's passion—
I want my heart that way, I think.
                 *   *   *

Later, back home, I toss crumbs to sparrows beneath the apple tree,
thinking of
        the great concrete and iron baseball stadium in Wisconsin
        how Lori and her family took me and my daughter
        to see the Brewers play,
        a well-gardened evening of uniform composition,
from the white-chalked lines, to umpires, to players' uniforms,
to the broad vista of infield and outfield clipped grass,
beautiful as a bride and groom taking vows,
        the scoreboard, cheers and boos of crowds,
        hot-dog hawkers and beer caterers,
        me imagining
        Little League kids whacking that ball
        skittering around bases—
game days that'll never be forgotten
just as acrobatic marvels on the monkey bars and swing sets
or the first time upturned in a canoe in a lake:
        fun times
        that transcend all our adult worries,
        experiences that tune our souls
        to a poetry always humming hound-howling our lives
            at the moon with joy.

Twenty

I've taken risks
starting as a kid
when I stole choir uniforms
from an Episcopalian church
so I'd have something to keep me warm that winter;
striding in six layers of robes through the streets
I looked like a biblical prophet.

                    *   *   *

When you turned up the ace you kissed the card
and when the joker scoffed at you
you were led away by authorities.
Second chances were for jive-time
nickel-diming chumps.
         It was beautiful,
in a way, to see us kids at seven and eight years old
standing before purple-faced authorities
screaming for us to ask forgiveness,
how irresponsible we were, how impudent and defiant,
              and that same night
in the dark all alone, we wept in our blankets
for someone to love—but we never asked for second chances.

Twenty-one

I am thirteen years old and waiting at the bus stop on
Barcelona Road, then semirural, newly paved, the cottonwood trees'
big leaves like farmer's hands, swung from tire ropes of wind, into
yards, ditches, rooftops, and porches. I had no idea about love and
I was attracted to those mid-school companion girls around the bus
stop whose cheap toxic perfume gave yard hens heart attacks and
burned the noses of dogs, who covered their snouts with paws and
yeowed. But I loved them, and although I was too shy to talk to
them and couldn't even look at them except when they weren't look-
ing at me, I loved their young thighs and calves, their sparingly
muscled hair and their avid eyes. These girls answered to no one;
they were the ones who would get pregnant at sixteen, ditch school
to roam the new mall, Coronado Center, smoke joints in the bath-
room, and work at minimum-wage hamburger jobs just to get out
of the house where their drunk step-dad beat on Mother. They
couldn't afford anything except love, and their hearts were warm
doughnuts dipped in the hot liquid in loins of midnight cowboys.

They were the girls who got fired from job after job because they stayed too long kissing boyfriends or flirting with customers. I basked in their disgust of the world, their contempt for "good boys," and even though they looked at me with eyes full of question, wondering why I couldn't speak, and even though I would have bitten the heads off frogs to prove my love to them, I couldn't speak because I had been taught not to. And there were other tougher guys around, who carried switchblades and wouldn't hesitate to throw you in front of a car if you insulted them. And the girls were theirs. These were the guys who got suspended every other week.

And there I was at the bus stop, fresh out of the orphanage and rippling away as the astounding world unfolded endlessly, and in the middle of the ripple I was a speck, a water strider riding the wave. The only reason I was going to school was to eat. Not to learn, or because I had friends, but to eat. The yellow bus signified a connection to society, a place to go and meaning in life. It was for me an arrival of the Holy Ghost because, when it arrived and I sat down, I had someplace to go. I didn't know that beyond Barcelona and Franzen Road, the cross streets where I lived—in a house with two cousins and an aunt and uncle who had decided to take care of me—that beyond the barrio and the blackboards and black birds in the cottonwoods, beyond the sun as if in a science-fiction novel, there were people in high places planning my life, how much I would make, what I would become, what my journey in life would be.

In New Mexico, until recently and with some exceptions, most judges, lawyers, school principals, and police chiefs were foreigners from other places. They treated me as if I were a mistake, a war detainee assigned a crime I didn't understand; I was held hostage, buried alive, and my only reprieve from rules and regulations and duress was the school bus. I didn't know I was a statistic, that a jail cell had already been built for me to fill, that most of the wrangling in courts between lawyers was not to treat me as an equal citizen but to determine how much freedom I was entitled to, not as much as the next kid, not the full freedom guaranteed by the Constitution, no, they were constantly deciding how much they thought they should allow me. I didn't realize that forces were at work practicing cultural cleansing, or that biological warfare imbued with benign rhetoric was funded in research programs at distinguished universities to prove I was inferior to others.

And looking out the bus windows I wanted to tell someone how much I loved America, how beautiful it was, how much I adored the Statue of Liberty for what little I understood her to symbolize, how I loved the dirt roads and dogs and people driving to work and others laughing on porches and others cooking breakfast, how I loved shopkeepers opening their doors and birds and ditch water and horses frosting the air with their vivacious snorts, yearning to gallop. I could never have dreamed that people were afraid of a thirteen-year-old boy they didn't know and that from this fear they murdered people who spoke up on my behalf—Martin Luther King Jr., Che, Robert and John Kennedy, Rubén Salazar, Joaquín Murieta.

I am speaking of a little boy who danced in the dark room, overhearing the old lady next door's radio playing a Bach concerto, and would turn in the moonlight coming in through the window and spin myself in the music. I didn't know how to play an instrument or read music and I didn't know anything about Bach, where he came from or what he was like, but the music cleared all that away and gave me a space in which to dance my small steps and make myself real in the dark, a phantom in my own opera. And my dance fell right in step with one of the qualities that make this country so great, its diversity. I added to its diversity, creating my own dance steps, yelping like a puppy at the notes that were like mother's milk at my lips.

Never would I have dreamed that in the highest quarters of American government I was considered a killer, a foreigner. That in children my own age the seeds of savagery were brewing; skinheads in Idaho 1993 would burn and murder others because they were different. I looked like the victims, black hair and brown eyes and olive skin. I could have never realized that in the eighties two presidents of America would fund research programs to search out proof my genes were prone to create monsters. Nor that as I walked ditches playing with grasshoppers, those pillars of society would be devising hate crimes against me, outlawing my language, and studying apes and monkeys to synthesize my customs with theirs and thus "scientifically" prove their hate hypothesis. I was a colonized enemy before I was born, and before acquiring language skills children learned to dream my blood bath, to believe I had no right to my ancestral lands or culture. Serbians, Muslims, Croats, Armenians, Azeris, Tamils, and Sinhalese, Greeks and Turks, Irish Protestants and Catholics, Israelis and Muslims, all slaughtering each other for domination and power, and lined up behind the warriors are the intellectual political scientists. All of it is justified historically, they say, and little did I know, when I was thirteen waiting for the bus, that eventually the ride would take me into a world filled with much more hatred.

In my yellow bus I felt safe but confused. I had no superstitions to keep phantoms at bay. The terrors of the world impinged upon my world. La Llorona crept at night along ditches, snatching children and devouring them. She originates from a historical legend of an Indian woman who chose to drown her children rather than let them be taken back to Spain by the Spaniards and taught to be European. I know that when I was born my heart was no larger than a sparrow heart, the size of a clam beating in its bone shell, still hearing the primal oceans of universes roaring in me.

No numbering system (4444) to give me pertinence, no card readers or dice or priestly blessings or medicine man or healer woman cleansing, I depended on the simple natural universe like leaves budding, long-legged spiders water-walking on culvert scum, the brilliant sky with its glittering stars, the simple ranchers living in trailers, whose fearless children rode horses, got kicked, ran back and forth from corrals, full of gusto and hearty openness, the dirt roads and mountain gully washes we call arroyos; I leaned heavily on the goodness of good people, filling my plate with fried potatoes and red chile con carne and beans; hot coffee, old cars rusting in prairie fields riddled with bullet holes and broken windows, deer hoofprints in pine-needled and piñon-shelled ground; and I dreamt while riding the bus of playing basketball under a light in the dirt lot, the backboard a makeshift piece of plywood, the netless peeled rim nailed haphazardly but firm to the board, and me throwing the ball up until I was tired and slept in a cot with four other cousins in the same small room, all of us smelling like dust and prairie resins.

I was part of a history and region deep in legends, songs, poems, corridas, and *danzas,* and riding the yellow bus I looked at images that reflected my identity—streets, buildings—and there was nothing but the workers of the world sweating and I realized very early that their sweat would be my song, that their smells and dirty work boots and women's laughter, all fighting in some peaceful and soothing way, patiently burning for civil liberties, for equal justice and respect, not what others were willing to give, one-quarter justice, one-half justice, but to break open the confines of all the intellectual rhetoric and give all people what was due them, equality and love and peace. And on that yellow bus in my own silence, watching the other kids throw spit wads and curse and feel girls and girls feeling up the guys and kissing and threatening others to fight, I dreamed new definitions for myself and my potential, because more than anything else I was a loving soft child, full and brimming and spilling over with sensitive romance and love and endeared to humanity, trying to reclaim a murky past filled with war and murder and betrayals, trying to see myself as what I was supposed to be.

And my heroes and heroines were those people never given their due who when I was young were getting on with the work of angels. There were barrio children my age dreaming, a thousand of them dreaming as I was, and on their journey most of them died. And the seeds in them opened such pain, such unbearable excruciating anguish, that they fell into alcohol and drugs, and the best minds of my generation put pistols to their brains and pulled triggers, hurled themselves off cliffs and slashed their wrists, pushed the heroin needle's plunger in and knew they were overdosing; there was too much pain and hell and abuse and darkness, their hearts had broken off and nobody in life had ever met them halfway or given them an iota of respect or opportunity; filled with grief and hurt they killed themselves so early and innocent and full of love and silence, and those who lived carried the memories of those who died young, and with promises and vows and to the heroic corpses that lined the cemetery lots, the living started the Movimiento, started writing books and painting murals, formed intellectual aesthetics, went on a search for their spiritual homeland, sculptors sculpted the demons and angels in their hearts exorcising the evil in our blood, praising the sweetness in us, bursting boundaries of ourselves, crossing la frontera back into Mejico to do peyote and drink sotol, do hallucinogens and roam in Mayan ruins at night trying to communicate with their ancestors; and others marched and protested, holding up the cross in one hand and the sword in the other, dying on the front lines for their civil rights, and the seeds of self-determination were born in thousands of kids riding yellow buses to schools that didn't give a damn about us.

And riding the yellow bus I sensed my heart beating under the hot pebbles, I sensed I was a foul sinner and an angelic saint, I began to sense that my power was as unending as all the grass blades and gravel in the world, a voice and vision in me began to erupt and niagara down in glistening growls sniffing at my roots on this land, that went down and down and down, bursting all the borders and creating bridges between me and the universe.

And when the bus stopped and started, my window was a yellow camera and the stopping and starting were shutter speeds as I shot photos of my world in the darknesss of my soul, knowing I would someday return to the darkroom and expose the photos to the universe through the blood acids of my sensibilities.

And auroras of energy whirled around common weeds, elm trees, misted off ditch water, shivered in the horseflesh quivering to get flies off, steamed from the bean pressure cookers, permeated the presence of adults who told me I was not wanted or needed, in the saliva spit bubbles I played with on my lips and tongue, in cussing and the hissing of fried potatoes, in the brown-bean-soup ditch water, in the buzzing of bus and bicycle tires whirring like angel's wings— the energy of creativity buzzed and came from everything, of resistance and the birthing from my dirty fingertips were the prints of Aztlan, of the real America, and though the books didn't carry the word or affirm the reality, bilingual people spoke of the barrio, and men and women tattooed their flesh in sacred calligraphy of our heritage—saints and legends and symbols and songs and names and places—and though the books at school had none of this I was schooling myself on that yellow bus, watching listening, learning *calo, huelga, mestizaje, pachucon,* Indio/Chicano *bato,* La Virgen de Guadalupe, Agila, *placas, ¡La Raza y q-vo! ¡Y-que! ¡Dar le gas!*

And in me the strange winds of time raged, religion and language and humanismo roared like a woman in labor in my gut, and I screamed that I wanted to be part of life! Not a splinter, not a rusty railroad spike driven down in creosote hells of society never to move or express myself; I wanted to wreak havoc and explode with love and crying and weeping in my own horrible dance of need to live and be accepted.

And on that yellow bus, with no friends and no place to live and no books, school, destinations, I created a part of the person writing this years later, gasping at the violence around me, lonely at night, reading books, wondering about my passage through time and how much time I wasted and how much more I wanted to do, how I scarcely touched the tip of my vision to make this planet and its peoples more loving and accepting and patient and enduring.

Twenty-two

I, like most people, am trying to change my life.
    I want it bull-vibrant
    charging full face into the sword.
I've had it with soap-opera
    privileged literary superflies,
        who enter the arena of fashionable trends
        like prancing Arabian geldings.
And after the dancing is done,
pastured, bred for good stock, bloodlines and lineage
    true and tested never to whinny a word against the master,
    obey the trainers, canter and cavort
    in soft raked sawdust arenas,
        and after, to nap
        in air-conditioned stalls on feather-filled comforters.

I wake up unshaven and exhausted,
grizzled with frustration over lack of money to pay bills,
        watching other poets zigzag in and out of traffic in new cars,
            wind in their shampooed hair,

neck and fingers dazzling with diamonds,
radio blasting Tupac Shakur,
on their way to a vegetarian café
and then off to the spa
to keep that figure pristine sixteen.

But there is another kind of poet I've known,
am blessed to have as a friend,
who picked me up from O'Hare airport in Chicago,
who had been through everything
unimaginable
and endured it, growing like a blueberry tree
with leafy grace in her gestures and rotund laughter
heady with mysterious gaiety in her eyes,
raped by a policeman,
as her man was murdered by the FBI in cold blood
who retreated to the mountains to care for her daughter
nourish her own soul with light, and retrieve
that crystalline innocence of the dewdrop again in her tears,
that poured many a night to douse the flames of her rage and agony.
Yes, I know that woman;
she drove me from Chicago to Milwaukee,
picking me up and
driving me three hours
late at night,
even renting a new truck for my stay
because her car was old and might break down,
working as a professor getting paid half
what her counterparts made,
working twice as long and seeing her at the table,
when her students of every race and color joined us,
seeing how they loved and respected her,
how she adored each one and lavished them with
her attention
but was seldom invited to read her work;
she was a commoner of the sort who make this world
habitable, effusing it with the spirit's splendor,

misting our darkest secrets and lonely memories
with the fog one sees close to rivers
>   that light burns away
>   to disclose a wondrous landscape
>   of fields and streams and mountains.

She was that for me,
living in her small apartment with her birds and plants and
>   Christmas lights
festooned over the kitchen door archway and window frames,
rising early to make tortillas for her students,
creating lovely cards to send to friends, that hit the receiver's hand
like corn seeds sprouting in the moist soil of a farmer's row.
Blessed to know this woman,
>   blessed to have her friendship,
>   blessed am I to be her friend,
who says of her life, It's a Chicago thing.
Frida Kahlo eyes,
black thick luscious hair, wonderfully full breasts,
and lips as succulent as ripe peaches,
>   her paintings hanging in every room of her apartment,
>   stations of the cross she recorded on her journey from
>   hell to mountain peak,
>   cherishing in her heart the faces of people she's known
>   and loved,
>   painting their portraits in the flesh and womb and heart
>   of each painting,
I awed at her healing, her magic, her life, her heart,
her healthy deep raucous laughter bordering each day
like pine trees in the distant horizon,
>   releasing eagles, hawks, timid creeks,
>   solace to weary travelers like me.

Thank you, *mil gracias mi compañera en la lucha*
de tener una vida honorable y llena de amor y alma,
¡Que dios te bendiga!

Your life a Chicago Thing,
        a Chicago Thing, you said,
                smiling with love at me.

Twenty-three

After night school
I enrolled in the university.

In between classes of American history,
I was escorted to the hills by police,
stripped, butt-ended with rifles,
and left bloody
and unconscious in dust and cactus.

In between classes
I tried to intercede between two cops
beating a drunk at the Blue Spruce bar.
I was cuffed, clubbed, jailed,
thong-slapped on thighs and heels,
by twelve Albuquerque jail officers
I cursed and refused to cower before.

In between semester breaks,
cops beat me in their car,
drove me to the edge of town,
to a hog-slaughter holding pen,
and boot-stomped me speechless,
(two holding me while each one
took their turn).

The barrio held different classes,
with more unruly police

as lecturers.
Had to miss university classes
weeks at a time
to let my puffy eyes and
swollen lips heal.

I flunked astronomy,
a study of the dreamless cosmos.
In psychology
pain became pleasing to me
when I walked out of class,
ashamed I couldn't answer the test.

I dignified pain with a smile,
an ancestral hand-me-down cure,
dignified it with a smile
in the last row,
in the back of class—
invincible.

My smile was the lizard
that quivered
on the classroom windowsill,
squirming close to the edge
for security.

My attendance
was low—almost always late,
embarrassed to enter mid-class,
I'd go to the campus duck pond,
sip coffee, and stare at a drunk
asleep on the bench. In the want-ad section
of the paper he slept on,
an employment agency
advertised for extras in a Redford movie
filming in northern New Mexico.
A grimy corpse. From his worn shoes

stray-dog spittle dripped,
pawing and greeting
recognizable smells of a trash can.
I was afraid of the drunk's face,
slouched with humiliation and defeat.
He stirred from his concrete sleep,
numb weight of his body
a dark crack slowly opening,
as I offered him what was left of my coffee,
cigarette, and some pocket change.
His decrepit smile was a signature
on his execution papers in a month or two
        from cirrhosis of the liver.

Twenty-four

White is an attitude of arrogance
        white comes in colors,
        white is a state of mind
it allows attorney generals and presidents to commit crimes
        white is a bat of an eye at children murdered in El Salvador
        white is the Iran Contra affair
white is the deaf ear and white is press censorship
        the white rain of pesticides
        the white bullet in Martin Luther King's heart
white are the contract papers to store nuclear waste at WIPP
white is a state of mind, not color
white are machetes, slicing ankle and knee tendons to cripple
those who would stand and confront
white are the handful of families who own most of the wealth
        white is cocaine
        white is heroin
        white is factory pollution

white are the laws and marble of justice buildings in
    Washington
white are interrogation lights, execution papers, not people
white are the eyes of the *desaparecidos* in Argentina.
White is the plume of atomic smoke mushrooming in Hiroshima
    and bellies of dead fish
white is an attitude isolated from all colors, exiled from the rainbow,
white are smiles of freshly barbered politicians on Capitol steps
    white are the fangs of jaguars behind zoo bars
    white is an attitude that disrespects any differences,
    white is the blank page an illiterate cannot fill
    white is the smoke from furnaces at Treblinka.
And white is the raging face full of solemn revenge
    white are gravestones,
    white is the place you escape to when you escape yourself,
    white are steer skulls in Santa Fe shops,
    white is an attitude that allows children's ribs to protrude
        from skin
white is the drooled mucus of a rabid dog foaming for blood,
white are scars on so many wrists from handcuffs.

    Refusal is brown, resistance is red, courage is golden,
integrity is bronze.

Twenty-Five

As a student,
after class,
I wonder
why I should be here,
and Davil in jail when he was so much smarter.
I remember in the county jail,
when I daydreamed on my bunk

of the life I have now.
I dreamed it was much more than it is.

In my other life,
seasons changed by what I heard and saw in the barrio,
not semesters and calendars.
Ax swings at dawn
were unspoken opinions of weather to come.
I unlearned what I had learned the previous day
to stay spontaneous and creative—
each filament of my spirit
my palm made a fable of—
in real life.

Now these sobering duties . . .
each book a grimed window-glass pane
effused with nebulous luster of words,
through which we try to discern life.

Before, my hands tried to dismantle
the tooth-edged wheel of life,
that splintered my youth
into a rash awakening of poverty, violence, and drugs.

The faint light of daybreak
collapsed inward
from outside pressure
and hardened my heart into
an immovable core.
I responded to
and fused to the instant of survival
in a heat-flash cry for existence
and diffused myself
like the raw material of a new star,
and the melody of my blood
cut and carved justice and values
as if they were log and stone

in deep-forest mineral compositions.
I was a mythical figure once.

Now that I have settled for security
and comfort, the pages I grade
whisper the language of emotionally dying men,
imprisoned women, with stagnant spirits . . .
who are deaf to gunshots
a mile from here,
where rookie guards target-shoot.
Bull's-eye hearts of dummies bleed
shredded cardboard. Shots echo
through Davil's cell window.
He thinks of
        Beltrán, Flores, Galviz,
        Garza, Morales, Prieto y Rodriguez,
        Santome, Torres y Vasquez—
            dead Chicanos
            brutally beat
            and murdered.
Their deaths
are tiny splinters of hurt,
slivered glass in every pore
of my skin, in my mouth, ears, and hands.

Twenty-Six

The end of October has always bored down deep in my blood.
The rapid speed of change. Twirling leaves
and great golden bruises of treetops. Everything
is associated, related to each other.
Brittle constructions creak out. The gray luster
of tin barns at dawn. The inward growth of colors.

Fence wood blackens, field weeds whiten, the air shimmers cold
into the lungs and against cheeks. The mare
gallops, tail arched, bucking, neck reared,
across the field.
I make soup, salad,
and a squash dish as kids run through the kitchen.
My tools lie dormant:
hammer, saw, rake, shovel, and others, like thick roots
hardening in the dusty shed. I track mud into the kitchen.
I pour myself a cup of coffee
and notice how
everything gives an opinion of itself during October.
The trees tell stories, tales of losing everything and going bravely
into the gray morning alone. Birds assess the air
like wine tasters. The intuition of things smolders forth and the pebbles
in the driveway celebrate the ancient rereading of eternal cycles—
the stones are hard bulging eyes attached to the top of the earth—
they are the eyes of the dead that have floated up,
and during the month of October
I can see them peer at me from behind the fallen leaves
as I walk along the path.

Twenty-Seven

Barrio Southside—
it's not like tourist postcards
sold in Old Town,
it lacks the flavor of proud heritage
that towns in Mexico or Spain have.
When it rains young boys carry roses in their teeth
while riding their bicycles
and their dogs scatter pigeons bathing in rain puddles
in the street.

La Vega, Vito Romero, Isleta: these are the roads
Chicanos take,
like the ancient tribe of Aztecas
searching for a new home to build their future.
Conquistadors armored in '57 Chevys
low-riding and panting fumes,
high on *carga* or *mota*,
the knife or gun in their pockets warmed and cuddled
like an infant in hell.

Bear the flames, brother Luis,
who still lives with his parents at forty-eight,
and who goes to church every Sunday, then
to Mike's Bar, to drink and fight the Lord's day
to a bloody end.

Bear the flames, Tito, sixteen years old,
playing chicken with a .38 last week
with your older brother
in your living room, until your boredom
boomed in the quiet afternoon sunlight
splattered with your brains
like fine powder in the weedy fields floating on the air.

Bear the flames, Eric,
who ripped off a jacket two weeks ago
from Mieyo's truck
parked outside my piñon picket fence,
and when confronted, wearing the jacket, tells Mieyo,
"Call the cops, I don't care!
I am going to prison anyway!"
And struts off, a black glove with the fingers cut off,
he wears to signify loyalty and readiness
to die or be imprisoned for the laws of Southside Barrio.

Bear the flames, Julian,
county cops visit every weekend at 4 A.M.

as you beat against the door, drunk,
screaming obscenities at your children and wife.

Bear the flames, Miguel,
arrested for DWI numerous times,
hustling spare tires and *gramitos de coca*
to buy eggs and dog food for your pit Diablo.

Bear the flames, Flaco,
stabbed a month ago with a bear knife
on North Fourth at the Corral,
when drunk, a *puta* lured you outside
to the parking lot, where an accomplice
sent the blade to the hilt through your chest.

Bear the flames, the bad flames
of addiction, Mario,
not as famous as the Kennedy or Belushi boys,
but cocaine and heroin has been your high
since sixteen.

Bear the flames, Perfecto,
county agents visit every week
to hang a red tag on your door
for all the junk cars and trucks in your yard.
"*Que se vayan a la chingada,*" he says, and tears
the red tags up. And without a permit,
he builds walls, rooms, sells and buys old cars and trucks.
"I have been doing this since before those kids in office
were ever born!"

And Jessie Jackson came last week
to Southside Barrio,
the *chavalitos, vatos locos, abuelitas, madres,*
and even packs of stray dogs looking for free beans and tortillas
crowded around this black man to hear him say,
"You have a right! Right to speak Spanish in schools!

Right to your lands! Right to equal opportunity!
Right to get paid decent wages for working with your hands!"

The Southside Cholos Locos, about two hundred *vatos*,
prowl at night with the right to kill
if you push them too far,
with the right to kill each other, to get lost
in the flames and die a brave death, a crazy death,
in the flames, burning,
with *I don't care, man! Let's get down!*
Louie's in the joint! Let's rob that store!
Fourteen, fifteen, sixteen, seventeen:
warrior children performing in the rites of fire,
to take life to the extreme, lose it all
in a bright all-flashing moment
as they soar to the darkness of death's lap,
and the parents like truncated old elm trees, gnarled
and dried, smoke roll-your-own-cigarettes on porches,
thinking how their sons and daughters could not endure
the long term burning and burning need
for dignity, freedom from poverty . . . they could not do it.

And if you get past the flames,
the burning,
if you learn to become a fire doctor,
understanding the way things work in this world,
then scarred from the flames
and strong with burning needs,
you awake to the destruction of broken chairs,
cracked walls, bad memories,
dead friends, no money, screaming children,
the last warning bills from the utility companies to pay,
the broken car, the things that need to be done
and never are,
you awake to all this and smile,
because you are alive, and it will be done,
it will be done, it will be done.

Just endure.
And endure.
Endure.

That's what the Old Town postcard
on the black wire rack would say,
to all the world—China, San Salvador, Cuba,
Mexico, Ireland—*Endure!*

And in the picture all our faces would be stern
and there would be empty black spaces
representing those dead ones
who have become ashes.

Twenty-eight

Poetry's mission is to subvert, to question, challenge, pro-
voke, to flail one's vulnerability and voice in the marvelous whirl-
wind of poetry's awe, flagging at the horns of the raging beast that
is society's gluttonous comfort, its obscene satisfaction with itself,
herding young minds to doubt the heart's compassion, trampling
those who would object, goring others who do not surrender, as it
fattens itself on the lush springs of employment paychecks.

So I have no money, and it's not on purpose or planned that
I find myself constantly ill at ease with finances. I never know what
lies beyond the next curve in the road; all I have are my meek con-
victions that serve well the spiritual traveler I am. I do not mind
finding myself stranded in silence. Crowds have booed and cursed
and attempted to knife and strike me for poems I read that upset
them. I have walked off more than one committee whose purpose it
was to hand out money to writers. Their agenda differed from mine,
in that they sought to follow the whimsies of fashion and not the

tenets of poetry that dictate themselves in the poem and the taste of the affluent leisure class. I please no one if it means I must whore the poem on every street curb that has a bank. If white men do not like the fact that, for the most part, they have chosen to remain ignorant of the literature of people of color or the oppressed, if publishing houses choose to stifle young poets by publishing feeble academic poetry, if slogan-sneering radicals do not believe in love poetry, I care not a flea's mustache hair what they think. Because poetry declares itself in every gasp of first breath a newborn infant inhales, in every note an opera singer manages to sing, in every black feather from a crow that shimmers in the afternoon sunlight, in every curl and bubbly spout of river water running downhill, in every young girl's tear and young man's cry for passion; poetry weaves its way in and out of our daily lives and will not—cannot—be denied by lip-puckering *tch-tch-tch* pseudo-podium officeholders and crowd-pleasing pedants.

Just yesterday I went to a prep community school, designed to take in sixteen- through twenty-one-year-old kids who have dropped out of regular schools. In return for a talk in the gymnasium and a workshop later in Mrs. Taylor's class, I was paid $200 and given a bag with a loaf of Italian bread, a bowl of cooked beans, and golden and red leaves Mrs. Taylor had picked from her yard. I heartily and thoroughly enjoyed the beans and bread at my apartment later, since my refrigerator was empty. And with the money I paid an overdue phone bill. Before that I visited the Colorado State Prison for $100 and spoke with convicts. After that I went into Denver and visited three elementary schools for $200. The brakes on my vehicle were completely gone, and the $200 went to fix them that same day. The children cried out delightfully when I told them they were the poets of tomorrow and to express themselves vociferously, and when they cried out they were important and they were poets, stars fallen like snowflakes from the ceiling, drenching each of our hearts with light from the human heart. I am simply following in the tradition of Walt Whitman, Hart Crane, Pablo Neruda, Lorca, and Rilke, and fuck the rest who sniffle and murmur ill-gotten gossip behind soft palms in the hushed rooms of academia or corporate America or city hall, because true poetry and poets will never succumb to the idle prattle and super-fly eminence that occurs when the poet panders to public taste.

Crate the little moralist brats and send them to deep-freeze storage.

Affirm poetry at any cost.

Twenty-nine

I lived in an old Victorian clapboard, trim-fringed
with flowery garlands, spiral staircase, milk-paned front-door glass.
A cemetery behind the house.
Checkered fields, rumpling in blue and yellow and buttoned with
    cracked shacks.
Grubbing country. Country of suicide
on full-moon nights.
On the porch my nephew aiming on the crosshairs
of his new BB gun
shot the right eye out of an owl in the tree in the front yard
at night.
        It dropped, a lead arrowhead on the end of a plumb line,
        full of death, gray wings dazed
        grasped helplessly for air—
        once an ally, air became its enemy—
        it careened in dirt at the foot of the tree.
I was horrified when my nephew called me out to ask my help!
        "What should we do, Uncle Jimmy?"
        Its right eye splintered into a ribbon of jellied blood
        reflected in its moon slime red mirror
        our meaningless violence.
I tasted this stupid act
        chalk on my tongue

as if I had opened a coffin and stuffed my mouth with
     bone dust.
I could hardly breathe. My young nephew, taught to shoot at
   anything that moves,
listened as I told him the owl's eye is his soul
one of two, it carries, and taking the right eye
destruction would now follow.
               We were scared
               confused
               as he held the owl
               blood dropped on the bare board
               porch
               under the porch light;
               at our shoes
               warm feathers
               exuded omen of evil to come.
          Its claws were underground stalagmites
          its beak a spiritual cutting knife.
          Suddenly the darkness counted our graces
          we held it as coins divided between thieves
          and the coldness of the hour left us alone, bitterly numb
               with the act.
"We must let him go."
There are things you don't doctor: no vet, no forgiveness for
   some acts.
The hillside beauty contoured in dark folds
gave up a minty fragrance of black spring ground worming
   awake.
          "Let it go."
          Bloodletting owl's eye
          is a world with no axis,
          is a boat at sea with no man;
          in the owl's bloody eye
               I saw
               smoking mirror
               plumes of gray smoke
               making my eyes cry.

It was not
till a few nights later
that my sister and her husband sat playing cards
in the parlor
while I sat upstairs typing away
and through the floorboard cracks
smoke unfurled.
I heard my name cried, then screams,
and when I ran downstairs
the house was gagged in smoke
and the smell of burning picture frames;
smoldering couch wood
crackled beneath my shoes.
Standing outside, watching the house burn,
I saw the owl's eye
throw its golden glare over the cemetery, over our face,
bronzing our guilt and the night a baroque plaque
etched with blossoming trees, white headstone, flagstone walkway
and four people standing arm in arm
at distance from the flames
guilty of the deed.
        Everything we had was destroyed.

Arc of cleansing fire
cackling through recent brush memory
towering heat
        giving back the sight of our frailty
        and how little we really know.
        I gripped my nephew's hand
        looked down in his face
        I knew his eyes saw the owl's eye
        in the flame—
        this house fire had given back to the owl
        an eye
        he took.

                    * * *

We walked down the dirt road,
an emptiness of wrong filled us.
My sister, hysterical, fled into the alfalfa fields and danced
       twirled and twirled by herself,
       then she rushed to the cemetery
       and sat, back to a headstone, and wept.
I followed her, patted her sobbing shoulders,
       praising what we had lost
       as an event to start over
giving the fire a prayer, a cleansing prayer.
       Rubble of ash smoldering behind us
       a feathery incantation
       of a lost eye
no amount of technology could repair . . .
       only something in the heart that tells us
       all life is as valuable
       as ours.

Thirty

       In Mexico a group of poor artists
pitched in their money and bought a crumbling four-story
and converted it into studios accommodating artists
from all disciplines—dance, painting, poetry, sculpture.
       For my reading in the gallery,
old imperious women sat stiffly in the front row on hardback chairs
hands properly folded on laps
and flanking them along the walls were barefooted girls and boys,
and in the chairs behind the old women were chin-shimmering men
black-haired heads glistening with hair tonic.
The young women wore feather necklaces and turquoise-stone
   wing bracelets;

their dark hair terraced,
falling into smooth waves over shoulders into sighing dark storms.

      After I read,
porters in purple vests wheeled in carts of whiskey, beer, and wine.
Delight blew through the gallery, their wings were testing the air,
the people rose, gliding into conversations,
when suddenly a young man came up to me.
      "I wish you to come with me and meet others in my group,
        will you meet with us?"
His shoes didn't have shoelaces, tongues sticking out, he wore a
    rope for a belt
to keep his loose faded jean pants on.
His impassioned plea was stripped of pretension.
      "Yes," I said.
      "Are you ready now?"
      I nodded and followed him down a flight of rickety
        wooden steps
into the chipped brick courtyard. The night filled
with frying foods and sewage and cheap perfume and *corridas*
and cries of vendors beyond the courtyard,
the moon, a bronze medal on a chain of clouds,
dragged itself along the red bricks.
      Nightlife sparkled a fuse; a fizzle of colors, smells, and sounds
swarmed crisscrossing streets thick with whore perfume,
field-working music, legions of street-corner
refugees, armless and legless beggars.
We shouldered past hundreds of people and finally, at the corner
    of a park,
an old beat-up battered car drove up; he opened the door and I
    got in.

      The thrust of immediate acceleration pushed me back,
I turned around and got scared.
There were three men in the back, including my host.
Their kind detachment concealed their wishes, none smiled;

they looked directly at me
the way a dog looks at a bird in a tree, seeing through me,
then one by one extended their hands with pious formality.
The driver swept and swerved through traffic. Deep silence. I felt
inexperienced in their presence,
felt myself a vain profligate, my life spilled milk on a table
because they were clean, hard, strong, their silence
mature and mine weak,
their appearance ascetic and priestly.
We were now hurtling into the outskirts of the city, fewer and fewer
houses, ominous heavy-equipment lots strung with barbwire,
cinder-block buildings beaten into bad health,
loose wire spotlights throwing an eerie net over the dark steel doors.
Then we arrived. I wanted to go back to the city.

      We walked into a room where other men were seated in
        a circle
and we sat down. A large man, young and incredibly strong and
    handsome,
started handing out shot glasses of whiskey, his gestures restrained.
He was not accustomed to pouring whiskey in glasses.
He was not used to dainty and careful protocol.
By their sunburned leathered features
I assumed they had lived in the mountains a long time.
They had something of the coarse and innocent ruggedness
of mountain stone, sharp-faced, living on meager provisions.
Crusty shoes spit-polished and buffed, shoelaces broken and
    knotted, faded shirts
        stiff with starch, washed a thousand times in mountain
           streams
        intended to look new, the men shifted uneasily in chairs
great legs creaking the wood,
and after all the glasses were filled, my host started.

    "We want to know what you think of poetry.
Do you think it has any influence over changing society?

What is happening in America?
Would you be willing to take these books and papers back with
    you and spread
them among the academic writers and poets of your country?"
        The questions came faster than I could answer.
They had been born in revolution, from many countries in Latin
    America,
children fighting dictators and tyrants,
each one of them had come together
because their families were murdered and they were the surviving
    casualties
living in the mountains, still fighting
for their freedom and respect and right to live. We talked poetry
with laughter, reverence, and respect, discussing what it was
until dawn light struck the torn curtains
and I shook hands with each of them, embraced each of them;
then I was driven back to my hotel. I carried the stack of papers
and books I would hand out to friends—
        I realized the poet's strength lies in the people,
        in what their hearts feel and hope and pray and dream.

Thirty-one

The lizards are skittering along fence lines—blue-bellied, hearts
    in throats
pulsing weedy arteries,
and the plumed partridges, in pairs, each has a mate,
blend into the gray dead tumbleweeds
and bushy sages along the arroyo.
Have you tasted sage? We call it the sacred blanket for grand-
    mother—peyote—
but it's bitter to the tongue,

yet many a time when I was driving and couldn't keep my eyes open,
I'd have some on me and chew it, stick my head out the window,
caress my hair in the light drizzle as I prayed.

And prayer: thankfulness is what it's all about.
I come up on the mesa and thank the black birds on the mesquites,
thank the nameless flowers sprouting red and white and blue in
    the heat,
thank the Creator for all that's come down
on these poor shoulders, wobbling my knees with such sadness
that an operation is needed to repair the splintered bone caps.

You might be a stranger to yourself,
but I'm not—
I've been digging stones out of my heart such a long time,
biting each one to make sure I'm not throwing away gold,
no need to wear a tie to impress a white boy
and fancily flirt with a white woman,
no need for that, I've got friends all colors,
and I mix them up in my blood, their words
the pebbles in a creek bed shimmering and glinting
with their own beginnings to be human beings,
because so distant from their roots,
one becomes mean and ill-tempered, and if you visit
English museums in London,
you'll find gods are men of commerce and banking,
and I'd rather be bunking with cigarette butts in a ho'-n-pimp hotel
than point to the bank as my green-feathered tribal village.

Yeah, girl, what we need to do is sit down
and powwow—
leaving behind this heated pool and beautiful Mexican garden of
    mine,
leaving my dawn-early strolls as I water each sage and perennial,
each piñon tree, each evergreen that hollers to me
how sweetly life can be lived and nourished
and how there's room for everyone—

even you and me, at the table,
even others of my people coming back to Turtle Island
pillaged and stricken with mayhem
under the guise of Manifest Destiny—
they come nonetheless, crossing miles of choppered-air
bulleted distances,
carrying beat-up grandmothers, slashed with army bayonets,
children crushed by INS Gestapo boots,
they come heeding a deeper call than yours and mine,
buried in Mother Earth,
concealed from those who would betray her,
the poverty pimps,
the strutting and sliding, the smoking and singing,
they come in silence, humble, back to their roots,
to the land of Seven Caves, the land of the Crane,
our Motherland, our roots,
and no one understands that what was written in Mayan codices
cannot be stopped,
smelling of earth drenched in blood,
stinking of sweat in rich growers' fields,
reeking of pesticides, of hunger, of slavery, of being beaten
    brutally
and still desiring basic integrity by showing it to others.

Color never mattered, it didn't then
and still doesn't,
I love the color black, man, you should see me in a black
turtleneck,
sleek pants that snug up around my sweet ass,
how my brown limbs flow with swanlike grace on the air,
how my arms fit another sister's and brother's arms
for the rocking and cradling and loving.

Color never mattered,
except to the colorless,
the lost tribe seeking roots,
seeking their sacred colors,

their beads and feathers and songs,
now screaming in hatred death doom dungeon torturing and
   twisted
chemically induced self-destruction,
never trusting, seldom fair, often manipulative,
they dress in the fanciest suits to conceal their colorless anemia,
they cunningly score a win by cheating where they can,
they incessantly adopt and take what they don't have respect for
except to turn a nickel into a dime—

so woman, you are full of bursting beauty,
despite the false reliance on plaques, knock-kneed innocence,
pretentious deference,
you breathe and your breath by virtue of your wonderful soul
gives black-jeweled veils to every woman under the moon,
breathing
gives every maui warrior a gut-filled arrow-killing God cry
of victory where he be, you be, I be,
all convoluted in a fireball of love and courage and sublime
   spontaneity
hurling and soaring through the heavens above banks
and the six o'clock news—
woman, being who we are and living as we live
is no flip of the switch and we got *Bay Watch* lives—
who wants it?—our lives are never going to be resolved,
never going to find peace, and why should they,
we are poets and warriors, racists and pacifists,
and to say we're not racist is to deny we ever lived,
because this system and every institution in this country
teaches subtle invisible can't-touch-but-it's-there racism.

And all these white boys and white girls
off into brotherhood and sisterhood
can't even begin to be my brother and sister
until they deal with their own racism,
the hot and cold, the sweet and bitter,
the fat and thin of it—

isn't in Whitman or Emily's poetry,
it's in our lives *now*
and our reaching is a way of saying we're tired of it,
have to make something else happen,
have to stop accepting the betrayals
and the nonsense that we can't live in peace
and love because
coming from a homeboy, and a million like me,
there's no winning.
Not having the luxury of living in a quaint woodsy idyllic way,
not having the money or the means to do so,
we find ourselves on the freeways speeding by others
who flip us off, who look at us and seethe with hatred
at me for having my ol' '49 pan-head Harley low-rider,
coming up and passing them,
coming up and contributing my jewels to the land,
to the children,
coming up and offering better education,
art, dance, language,
and woman, that's the real world,
not the poetry crowds
gulping beer and clapping drunkenly,
not the fancy hotel soap and fragrant laundered clothing
we wear,
the truth is if you put your finger in my
sweet bronze-brown flesh you're gonna come up
with cups of the sweetest wine and such savory bits of heart food
it'll make your mouth pucker as if you bit a juicy golden peach.

Tired of them telling me
what's good and what's bad,
tired of the doubt about who we are,
tired of teachers teaching what they don't practice,
tired of the starched manners and lies of politicians,
tired of measuring a woman's worth or a man's strength
by the curves on her body and his—
listen to oldies,

humming them as I do on long prairie rides across the badlands,
going to my village
where richness is measured by your integrity and how you
    support your family
and poverty by your lies and false words.

For a very brief time
I wanted to be like them,
yet the heart-coal burned in the dark
with all the ardor and vehement desire to be me,
and all it took was a stand, take a stand,
no matter where you are,
no matter what road or paved yellow-brick dream,
no matter what path, a goat's or a queen's softened by strewn petals,
you can stand and be who you are—

Just have to accept the grief,
the tragedy,
the hurt,
the betrayals,
the unbelievable anguish of being me, you, us,
and make songs out of the blues, girl,
and you, better than most,
can sing them so as to make even
Snakebelly rise out of that grave behind a Louisiana prison kennel,
and burn the ears off them hounds,
the noses off their faces,
and have that fat little squat warden chewing his cowboy hat brim in
anxiety,
because there's no caging up the blues,
imprisoning the song in people's hearts,
none of that, no ma'am.

And what I sing to the world
is get up off that
"I haven't experienced the clubs and cages and bloody streets,"
because if not you than yours will,

a son, a daughter, no one escapes
another man's hatred, another woman's bigotry,
we all suffer it down the road a bit,
we meet what we most tried to hide from,
we encounter it when answering the door;
In one way or another,
the bill collector arrives and hands us the bill.

And the time for explanations is gone,
vapid and sordid self-flattery because we handle language so well.
I don't hear the cactus explaining itself,
nor the mimosa tree in the front yard saying why it is
the color it is,
nor the water as it streams downhill telling me it has to do so:
just is, just as we are and have been,
once we cut what we've been taught to believe,
get on our knees and hands and scrape up what we threw away
a long time ago, put back together that eggshell angel and prop it
on our shoulder, and by the winds and magic of our hearts,
it starts flapping wings and blessing us again.

And no,
there isn't room for the I'm-confused chants,
for the yeah-what-about-me snivels,
for the fear that comes from talking out
in places and in front of people
who pay your salary—that noose around my neck,
I chew right through that piece of limp frayed rope,
I saw through their words and found a nest of fanged lies,
I touched their flesh and it was colder
than an ice tray in the fridge—

no room for anything
except my beautiful sister, beautiful woman that you are,
to love yourself and sing your songs
that come from a river way below the stone and the fancy clad
    feet of the rich,

that black molten fire that is the tongue of all birthing origins,
that song that kept us alive,
that protected us against the predators,
the one our mothers hummed a thousand years ago
when they carried us
in a time when dinosaurs grumbled the blues.

Thirty-Two

I am
        a cut-tongued sparrow
                    perched on concertina wire barbs
                            that crown the dawn
                            with thorns.
Prisons scab the fields
beyond each city
        where even poets turn their backs
        on the deafening noise of cut-tongued sparrows.
Flesh and bones forced to speak in silence,
flesh used as paper to write upon,
flesh used as a battlefield
        to tear and puncture and gash and mutilate
but so resilient that gas chambers
and thousands of watts of high-voltage lightning
must be used to burn and scorch,
while on every utility wire
        vast flocks of cut-tongued sparrows
                    mourn with their bilingual warbling
                            the deaths of young prisoners.
Picture a painting
of sparrows
        flustering around a feeder,
                    embedded in each seed

a tiny razor
        that slices their tongue
                to silence their song.
Blood in the water,
    in the city,
            scattering blood
                    on the idyllic lotus blossoms
                    in the fountain pond.

We've sensed how the world is so inclined
        to serve the privileged
        and starve the poor,
but we do nothing,
        tsk-tsking
                the wasteland of corpses
                        on the evening news,
                        vowing to build higher walls,
                        vote more cops,
                        more prisons
as the cut-tongued sparrows
flutter at street-corner ledges
birthing demons that will maul the future, our children. . . .

Thirty-Three

Yesterday, I went to see this seventeen-year-old Dene kid
sentenced to thirty-five years
        hard prison time.
After I gave the keynote address
        to GED graduates,
        talking a little to the rest of the inmates
        on the bleachers, kids in khakis,
                crew cuts, tattoos.

A counselor asked me if I'd talk to Yazzi,
 locked down in high security.
   They brought him out into a small room—
   the counselor, the warden, a couple of guards—
   sneakers, T-shirt, and beige khakis,
   he trembled when our eyes met,
 he was me
 twenty-five years ago
 me with no hope, me with brown eyes,
 me, totally lost and confused and scared.
I told him he was not going to do those thirty-five alone,
I'd be with him all the way,
I'd carry him through the dark time, shoulder him
when despair consumed him,
we had to do this together, he and I:
  Yazzi and Jimmy,
   brothers in soul,
   and I didn't care what he'd done,
   there's nothing to be ashamed of,
he is my Dene brother,
and I'll inspire him to draw on *panos* (handkerchiefs),
write poetry,
  share his despair and dreams and love,
  be with him
   as if he were me and I were him—
both of us will track our demon footprints into us,
vigilantly waiting their appearance.

  Stay true to yourself, Yazzi,
  keep faith in your heart,
  rejoice quietly in your vision
   reconcile your soul with the Great Creator,
   let Mother Earth accompany you,
   take the bars and stones of your cell and prison walls,
   braid the stones and bars like beads around the
    plants and flowers

of your soul and heart,
pray hard, the hard prayers
that must pass your lips
with a lifetime of hurt
and shatter them with flowers
cracking stones.
You and I, prisons they transfer you to,
my poems will follow like wind-whirling laughter
to make you smile;
my poems will carry your foods, the aromas of Indian bread and
    corn and chili
savors reaching your nose, making you smile;
and my words will hungrily knock at your dream's door,
    offering you a rope to escape;
        I'll pull you up
                from the merciless brutality
                of prison time,
and our spirits tied together,
I will scream with you at your keepers
weep with you at the tragedies,
devoutly pray with you at night,
uttering forgiveness, begging blessings,
for humble sight to see through the long dark nights;
        two flames flickering in the windstorm,
        keeping each other lit when one goes out,
        as savage tears convulse from our eyes,
        I'll shake my head like a wild horse
                galloping freely through the prairies,
                letting go of remorse and guilt
                for wrongs committed.
We'll put those drug-crazed drunken days behind us,
we'll strengthen our conviction and integrity,
we'll not wallow in self-pity,
we'll respect our pain and hurt,
and we'll stay the course, good brother, cherishing our love of life,
        our volcano souls
        the source of fire beginning,

the original source of the waterfall's innocent leaping and feeding
     rivers—

You and me, Yazzi, we'll make it!
          We'll have our modest rewards and humble achievements,
          we'll appreciate what our senses absorb,
          we'll stretch our minds over the land
          like a night sky discovering new stars,
          wandering as dreamers in search of connection
          to the fire, for a place to rest, one warrior
          to another warrior.
Listen to me—
          we can shape our sadness
          into a tree,
          our tears into white/black eagle feathers
          our hurt into hawk claws,
          our hope into hummingbird beaks,
and even at times we'll fly so high we'll bruise our skin against
     the sun,
we'll bathe in the moon glow, having never felt so much freedom,

Stick with me, Yazzi,
          we can do it;
          we can dance our birthing thanks between light and dark,
          we can merge the boundaries of freedom and imprisonment,
          we can piece the fragments of ourselves together again,
          we can transform the darkness into a lightness,
                    a succulence, that life
                    bites into making us part of all things,
                    opening our wings, you one, me one,
we'll fly together, a blur of beings, creating ourselves anew with
     flight!
Good brother, don't lose hope!

Thirty-Four

No matter how many poems you tear up,
no matter how you use all your power and money
    to quiet the voices of freedom,
    to diminish their poetry, to discredit them,
    to exclude them from your reviews,
    to burn their videos, to trash their audio tapes,
    to use language as a weapon to destroy their integrity,
    to label them, stereotype them as vulgar or obscene,
no matter how many academics you pay
to parrot your politics in book reviews and scholarly papers,
your fear and hysteria and accusations
will not silence their voices,
will not stop their words from reaching the people,
their free minds and golden spirits will always triumph,
will always be discovered
    by people struggling to live with honor,
    by dancers and singers seeking vigorous expression,
    by painters enchanted with color and metaphor,
    philosophers dazzled by original insight,
    and teachers who want to instruct without compromise.

@e.nosssthyyyyy
I Bounce out in
Abril